ROB GIBSON was born in Glasgow and brought up in Dennistoun. His early interest in Scottish history has encompassed both Highland hill walking and land reform. In 1972 he graduated from Dundee University with a degree in Modern History and, until 1995, pursued a teaching career in Easter Ross. Through his love of traditional music he has convened the Dingwall-based Highland Traditional Music Festival for twenty years and he has sung in several groups. Currently with the band Ceilidh Ménage, he has performed at festivals in Scotland and Brittany. He wrote the show *Plaids and Bandanas* for performance at the Highland Festival of 1998. It has played in the Highlands, Edinburgh and Borders and in September 2000 at eleven venues in Alberta, British Columbia and Montana.

Rob's interest in land issues has led to an active political life including working for eight years from 1988 as an SNP District Councillor in Ross & Cromarty. He has contributed to various journals over the years and has published several books including *The Promised Land* (1974); *Highland Clearances Trail: A Guide* (fifth edition, 1996); *Crofter Power in Easter Ross* (1986); and *Toppling the Duke – Outrage on Ben Bhraggie?* (1996).

Plaids & Bandanas

From Highland drover to Wild West cowboy

ROB GIBSON

Luath Press Limited

EDINBURGH

www.luath.co.uk

Acknowledgements

MY FELLOW PERFORMERS IN Ceilidh Ménage and Cowboy Celtic deserve a medal for helping me to develop this book from an array of facts and figures. So thank you, Lizbeth Collie, Jonathan Hill, Malcolm Kerr, Jennie Renton, Eleanor Scott and Jem Taylor in Scotland, and David Wilkie and Denise Withnell in Canada. Invaluable advice and information about Scots in North America came from writer Tom Bryan. Miranda and Iain MacDonald provided information on Dexter cattle and Doric songs. Thanks also to the Highland Festival that supported the production of the original show in 1998; to Charlie Beattie who was game to be photographed in the drover's gear; to the staff of Dingwall and Evanton libraries and to the Highland Cattle Society, who helped with my many enquiries; to all the sources of quotes and pictures that are duly listed in the text; to various readers who gave advice that helped produce a much better book. I am grateful to all who provided inspiration for this project, which has proved to have wider resonance than we first anticipated. Finally, a special thank you to Brian McNeile and Calum MacDonald for kindly granting permission to reproduce verses from their songs *Lads o the Fair* and *Rocket to the Moon* respectively.

First Published 2003

The paper used in this book is acid-free, neutral-sized and recyclable. It is made from low chlorine pulps produced in a low energy, low emission manner from renewable forests.

Printed and bound by
Bell & Bain Ltd., Glasgow

Typeset in 10.5 point Sabon by
S Fairgrieve, Edinburgh 0131 658 1763

Contents

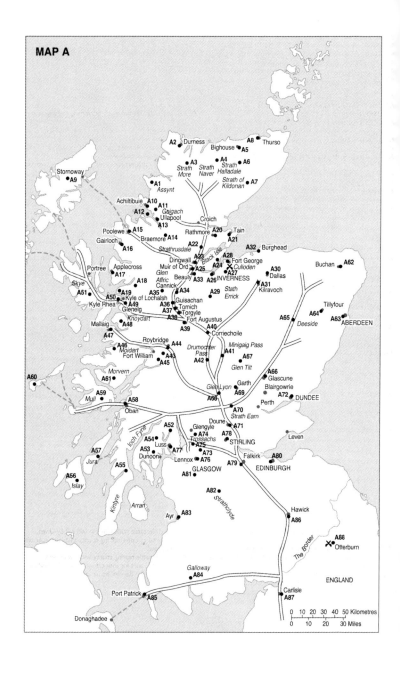

MAP A

Sutherland & Caithness

A1 Assynt: major clearances of 1812 inland straths for sheep.
A2 Durness: heart of the old MacKay province of Reay.
A3 Strath More: early home of herdboy Rob Donn.
A4 Strath Naver: brutal serial clearances by Patrick Sellar.
A5 Bighouse: seat of MacKay droving laird for whom Rob Donn worked.
A6 Strath Halladale: part of the Bighouse estate.
A7 Strath of Kildonan: cleared 1818-19, scene of gold rush 1860s.
A8 Thurso: sanctuary for some Clearances victims.

Ross & Cromarty

A9 Isle of Lewis: ancient source of black cattle.
A10 Achiltibuie & Polglass: home of migrant Celtic cowboys in Montana.
A11 Coigach: rugged peninsula where clearances were resisted.
A12 Loch Broom: safe harbour & stock raising district.
A13 Ullapool: 1773 departure point of the Hector for emigrants to Nova Scotia.
A14 Braemore: Lochaber cattle thieves caught here.
A15 Poolewe: old mainland port, imported cattle from islands.
A16 Gairloch: MacKenzie estates dominate crofting life.
A17 Applecross: 6th-century Celtic missionary base cleared for 19th-century deer forest.
A18 Kintail: cross-country routes reach west coast fjords here.
A19 Kyle of Lochalsh: railhead 1897, ferry for Skye till toll bridge built 1996.
A20 Rathmore: birthplace of Matador rancher Murdo MacKenzie.
A21 Tain: legal centre & market in 'Lowland Highlands'.
A22 Strathrusdale: attempts to drive sheep from Ross-shire in 1792.
A23 Dingwall: County town with livestock mart and rail junction.
A24 Black Isle: fertile peninsula with port at Cromarty.
A25 Muir of Ord: Am Blar Dubh, site of famous 19th-century cattle tryst.

Inverness-shire, Nairn and Moray

A26 Inverness: scene of Patrick Sellar trial, 1816.
A27 Culloden: battle site of Jacobite defeat in 1746.
A28 Fort George: Extant Hanoverian fort guarding north end of Great Glen.
A29 Strath Errick: old home of droving, song collecting Fraser laird.
A30 Dallas: 'Scotty' Philip, who saved American buffalo, born here.
A31 Kilravock: cattle raiding target of Keppoch MacDonalds.
A32 Burghead: huge Pictish fort where bull carvings have been found.
A33 Beauly: original cattle market that moved to Muir of Ord in 1820.
A34 Cannich: first droving inn for forty miles through deer forests.
A35 Glen Affric: ancient drove route and deer forest.
A36 Guisachan: former Chisholm lands turned to deer forest.
A37 Tomich: inn on Glen Cannich drove route south to Torgyle.
A38 Torgyle: point in Glen Morriston to which Cannich drove route descends.
A39 Fort Augustus: Hanoverian fort guarding roads to Corrieyairack and Glenelg.
A40 Corrieyairack Pass: drove & military road from Great Glen to Speyside.
A41 Minigaig Pass: drove route from Badenoch to Atholl.
A42 Drumochter Pass: main Inverness to Perth tolled drove route.
A43 Corriechoile: home of famous drover, John Cameron.
A44 Roybridge: Brae Lochaber gathering point for Larig Leacach drove route.
A45 Fort William: 17th-century fort guarding south end of Great Glen.
A46 Moidart: landfall and departure point of Prince Charles Edward Stewart 1745-46.
A47 Mallaig: West Highland railhead 1901 and port.

A48 Knoydart: Clanranald lands brutally cleared from 1750.
A49 Glenelg: fort, landing point of cattle swum from Skye.
A50 Kyle Rhea: cattle were swum to mainland from here.
A51 Isle of Skye: source of cattle, soldiers and scene of Crofters' War, 1882.

Argyll and Bute

A52 Arrochar: head of Loch Long, on drove route from Argyll towards Lomondside.
A53 Cowal: early area for improved farming and source of black cattle.
A54 Loch Fyne: Campbell heartland where Knockbuy improved black cattle.
A55 Kintyre: farm improvements featured dairy cattle shipping milk produce to Glasgow.
A56 Islay: black cattle producing island, now famous for Islay malt whiskies.
A57 Jura: cattle producing island, George Orwell wrote 1984 here.
A58 Oban: railhead 1880, port for southern Hebrides.
A59 Mull: island source of black cattle, much cleared, dubbed 'The Officers' Mess'.
A60 Tiree: source of black cattle and tenacious crofting culture.
A61 Morvern: cleared cattle country for sheep and stalking empires.

Eastern and Central Scotland

A62 Buchan: source of native 'humbies', in Aberdeen Angus breed.
A63 Aberdeen: major farming region, oil and fish port.
A64 Tillyfour: Wm McCombie successfully developed Aberdeen Angus cattle here.
A65 Deeside: Gaelic/Doric disputed cattle breeding area.
A66 Glascune: 1392 battle between locals and cattle raiding Wolf of Badenoch.
A67 Glen Tilt: cleared early for deer forest; blocked drove route in legal dispute.
A68 Glen Lyon: fertile Campbell glen on drove route from Rannoch to Crieff.
A69 Garth: home of General Stewart contemporary critic of Clearances.
A70 Crieff: home of famous cattle tryst 1690-1760.
A71 Doune: site of major livestock tryst in later 18th century.
A72 Dundee: industrial city, home of the Matador Co.
A73 Gartmore: Stirlingshire seat of Cunninghame Graham family on Argyll drove route.
A74 Glengyle: home base of MacGregor Clan chiefs.
A75 Trossachs: MacGregor heartland; Walter Scott's poems spawned Highland tourism.
A76 Lennox: fertile land preyed on by MacGregor blackmailers.
A77 Luss: Colquhouns lands raided by MacGregors and MacFarlanes in 1603.
A78 Stirling: 'key to Scotland', lowest crossing point of River Forth.
A79 Falkirk: top Scottish livestock tryst here 1760-1900.
A80 Edinburgh: Scottish national capital, source of credit for cattle drovers.

South-west Scotland and the Borders

A81 Glasgow: Scottish industrial capital and huge market for cattle and sheep.
A82 Strathclyde: cattle raided here in 600 AD by Urien.
A83 Ayr: capital of cattle rearing county that later specialised in dairy breed.
A84 Galloway: cattle rearing county, with own breed.
A85 Port Patrick: port for Irish cattle en route for England.
A86 Hawick: Border Reivers home on major Scottish – English drove route.

England

A87 Carlisle: English Border strongpoint on drove route to South.
A88 Otterburn: cattle raiders battle site 1388 when 'dead Douglas won the day'.

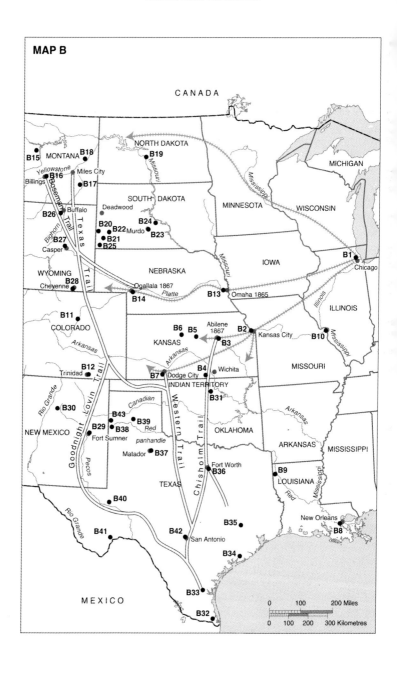

MAP B

CANADA

NORTH DAKOTA

B15 MONTANA B18
Yellowstone
B16 Miles City
Billings B17

Buffalo
B26
B20
Bighorn B22 Murdo
B27 B21
Casper B25

WYOMING
B28
Cheyenne

B11
COLORADO

B12
Trinidad

NEW MEXICO

B30

B43
B29 B39
B38 Red
Fort Sumner panhandle
Matador B37

B40

B41

B19
Missouri

SOUTH DAKOTA
Deadwood

B24
B23

NEBRASKA
Ogallala 1867
B14 Platte

B6 B5 Abilene
1867
KANSAS B3

Dodge City B4 Wichita
B7
INDIAN TERRITORY
B31

Canadian

Western Trail

TEXAS

B42
San Antonio

MINNESOTA

IOWA

B13 Omaha 1865

B2
Kansas City

MISSOURI

OKLAHOMA

Arkansas

ARKANSAS

B9
LOUISIANA
Red

B35

B34

B33

B32

MEXICO

MICHIGAN

WISCONSIN

B1
Chicago

ILLINOIS

B10

MISSISSIPPI

New Orleans
B8

0   100   200 Miles

0   100   200   300 Kilometres

USA

Illinois
B1 Chicago: rail centre, huge cattle processing centre.

Kansas
B2 Kansas City: rail and cattle processing centre.
B3 Abilene: McCoy used Chisholm Trail to found cattle market at railhead.
B4 Caldwell: railhead cattle town that superseded Abilene.
B5 Elsworth: short-lived railhead cattle town.
B6 Hays: short-lived railhead cattle town.
B7 Dodge City: buffalo killing centre and 1880s cattle town 'with its hair on'.

Louisiana
B8 New Orleans: early commercial centre and port.
B9 Shreveport: Mississippi River port for early cattle trade.

Missouri
B10 St Louis: rail & market centre.

Colorado
B11 Denver: State capital and rail centre.
B12 Trinidad: base for Murdo MacKenzie of the Matador.

Nebraska
B13 Omaha: cattle marketing centre.
B14 Ogallala: rail junction and cattle market.

Montana
B15 Great Falls: Charlie Russell Wild West artist worked here.
B16 Billings: cattle market & railhead attracted Highland migrant cowboys
B17 Little Bighorn Battle where 'Custer died a'running'.
B18 Miles City: livestock market & railhead.

North Dakota
B19 Bismarck: capital of North Dakota on main rail line.

South Dakota
B20 Belle Fourche: major cattle producing region.

B21 Black Hills: Indian heartland, gold strike causes flash-point.
B22 Deadwood: gold panning Mecca in Black Hills.
B23 Murdo: small railhead used for transportation of Matador beef.
B24 Pierre: town near Scotty Philip's ranch and buffalo saving operation.
B25 Pine Ridge: Indian Reservation and cattle grazing zone.

Wyoming
B26 Buffalo: capital of Johnson County.
B27 Casper: railhead for mid-Wyoming.
B28 Cheyenne: capital of Wyoming and of Stock Growers' Association.

New Mexico
B29 Fort Sumner: cattle sales point for Indian reservation.
B30 Santa Fè: capital of New Mexico.

Oklahoma
B31 Indian Territory: through which Chisholm Trail reached Kansas railheads.

Texas
B32 Brownsville: town near Mexican border.
B33 Corpus Christi: cattle centre in south Texas.
B34 Matagorda: peninsula where Col. Maverick's unbranded cattle flourished.
B35 Gonzales: Early Anglo ranches in this area 1830s.
B36 Fort Worth: many Texas cattle trails joined Chisholm Trail here.
B37 Matador: town named for ranching business of the area.
B38 Palo Duro: canyon base of Goodnight's JA ranch.
B39 Panhandle: north Texas area of big ranching fame.
B40 Pecos River: along which the Goodnight Lovin Trail swung NW.
B41 Rio Grande: border between Texas and Mexico.
B42 San Antonio: old Spanish town – scene of Alamo.
B43 Staked Plains: arid ranching land.

Canada (see Map C overleaf)
C1 Calgary: Alberta centre of cattle country.
C2 Lethbridge: important border post for Mounties.
C3 Swift Current: now Saskatchewan, land leased here by Matador Ranch.

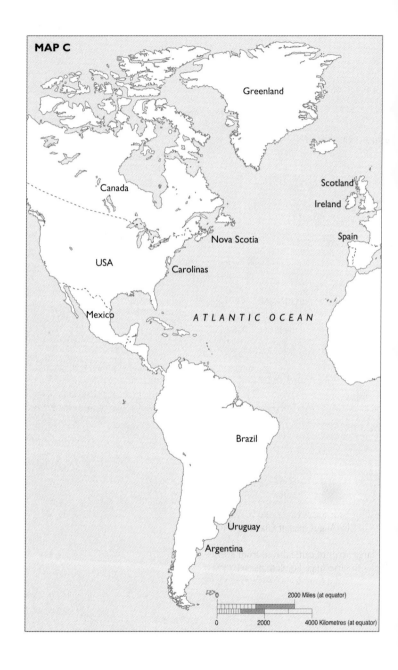

MAP C

Greenland

Canada

Scotland

Ireland

Nova Scotia

Spain

USA

Carolinas

Mexico

ATLANTIC OCEAN

Brazil

Uruguay

Argentina

0   2000 Miles (at equator)

0   2000   4000 Kilometres (at equator)

Chronology

Europe	America
	200,000 BC bison first reach North American continent via the land bridge from Asia; smaller American buffalo evolve from original stock to roam the plains and forests of North America
wild aurochs first domesticated 6,000 BC	
domesticated cattle reach Scotland and Ireland 3,500	
Celtic cattle herding well established 700 Celts dominate Western Europe for 1,000 years with their, iron swords, wheels and cattle culture mythologised in epic Tain Bo Cuialgne	
incised and bas relief Pictish stones show importance of bull motifs 400 to 800 AD Urien ruler of Death of Columba at Iona 597 Rheged raids Strathclyde for cattle 600 Picts and Scots merge as Alba 847 Scotland's border along Tweed established 1018	985 AD Viking colonisation of Greenland 1010 Viking leader Kalsefni sets up short-lived colony in Vinland [modern Nova Scotia], animals present include cattle
Scots cattle salesmen get safe passage to trade in England after fifty years of war - 1359 Scots exchequer records 50,000 hides exported 1379 Otterburn battle won by dead Earl of Douglas after raiding Northumberland cattle 1388 Wolf of Badenoch's cattle raid beaten off by Angus men at Glascune 1392	
large herds of cattle driven from north Wales to serve huge London market 1470 Cattle from Isle of Skye driven to Inverness market 1523 centuries of Border raiding ends as Scots and English united under King James VI & I 1603	1492 Columbus discovers Hispaniola and begins colonisation of America with people and livestock 1500 Norse colony in Greenland lost

Europe	America
last wild auroch killed in Poland 1627 incidents of cattle raid in Deeside recounted in ballad, *The Baron of Brackley* 1592 AD & 1666 Irish cattle banned in Britain 1667 last reported ritual cattle raid as Macdonalds invade Kilravoch, Nairn 1670 Scots Parliament authorises Earl of Perth to set up a cattle Tryst at Crieff 1672 Bank of Scotland founded 1695 cross-border cattle trade encouraged by Union of Scots and English Parliaments to sit in London 1707 successful cattle drover Rob Roy outlawed for 'absconding' with £1,000 of Marquis of Graham's cattle investment 1712 Coutts Bank founded and helps fund cattle trade 1727 Army Officer Capt. Burt deplores Highland tolerance of 'cattle lifting' 1730 death of famous cattle raider Rob Roy 1732 foiled Lochaber cattle raid at Lochbroom and pacification of Highlands after defeat of Jacobites at Culloden leads to sale of 20,000 head of livestock at Ft Augustus 1746 cattle rustling is rife & laws ban tartan, weapons and bagpipes but drovers exempt 1752 Crieff Tryst declines and Falkirk Tryst set up as cross-border trade increases 1770 rinderpest cattle plague across Europe 1776 famous drover John Cameron 'Coirechoille' born near Spean Bridge, Lochaber 1780 sheep farms set up in Highlands and resistance breaks out in Easter Ross in the Year of the Sheep 1792 Continental cattle markets cut by British/French twenty years of war. Increased demand to feed forces when 60,000 cattle were sold at Falkirk Tryst 1794	1521 first Andalusian cattle landed in Mexico by Gregorio de Vilalobos 1544 Spanish settlers begin Florida and Texas and ranching; cattle escape and breed in the wild becoming know as 'long horns' 1608 attempts to form English colony of Virginia begin and are sustained despite massacre, disease and famine from 1623; other colonies built on fishing stations in Massachusetts [Pilgrim Fathers], Nova Scotia Maryland, and Carolina had varying success in the 17th C Over three centuries Spanish missions and haciendas train Indians to be cowboys to tend their extensive herds and flocks. 1773 Emigration of Skye tacksman Sir Allan and Flora MacDonald to North Carolina with family and servants just before outbreak of war for American Independence in which he took the loyalist side, was captured and subsequently returned to Skye where Flora died in 1790. 1776 John D Chisholm emigrates from Scotland to join his father and family in South Carolina becoming successful traders and through marriage to Cherokee Indians a tirbal spokesperson. 1784 victory over British forces wins independence for thirteen original colonies of the United States of America. settlers push

Europe

red cattle from Glenlyon shipped to Hebrides to form distinctive Highland cattle breed 1802

poem Grampians Desolate warns of the decline of cattle and rise of sheep farming 1804

experiments begin to create the basis of the Aberdeen Angus breed 1810

trial and acquittal at Inverness of Patrick Sellar for Strathnaver atrocities in 1816

Countess of Sutherland forceably cleared over 5,000 cattle raisers from inland straths to wild sea coasts 1814-1819

cattle and sheep from NW Scotland sold at Am Blar Dhubh Muir of Ord Tryst 1820

Sir Walter Scott wrote tale of The Two Drovers 1827

twenty-eight Highland deer forests created for sport interrupt drove routes 1839

British Corn Laws repealed to usher in free trade in foodstuffs 1846

potato blight in western Europe leads to famine in Ireland and mass emigration 1845-1850

Gisbourne eye-witness account of Falkirk Tryst shows 100,000 cattle and over 200,000 sheep sold there in 1849

Coirechoile once the richest Scottish drover dies in poverty at home 1856

railway networks spread into Scottish Highlands and west Wales 1860

decade of rinderpest disease in Europe reduces herds to a fraction for meat consumption of rising industrial populations 1860s

breed developer William McCombie, Tillyfour wins top prizes for his Aberdeen Angus cattle at Smithfield Show, London 1868

growing concern in Ireland as American imports imperil Irish cattle trade to England and fuels land revolt 1877

US cattle imports treble in three years –

America

across west seeking new lands beyond the Appalachians into the Ohio basin.

1805 part Indian Jesse Chisholm born in Tennessee

1832 Anglo ranchers encouraged to settle in Mexican controlled Texas where Richard A Chisholm registers his brand at Gonzales. Jesse Chisholm sets up trading roads in Indian Territory [Oklahoma]

1849 Texas cattle driven to California to feed gold miners
Texas cattle driven to New York to drum up business

1856 Samual Maverick's name given to all unbranded cattle after his Matagordo County, Texas ran wild

1860 Lord South Esk's Aberdeen Angus cattle imported to Ontario

1861-1865 US Civil War disrupts ranch development in Texas and western Plains.

1865 north and south buffalo herds wiped out for tongues and skins only later as fresh meat for railroad workers

1867 first imports of live US beef to Liverpool causes food riots. Cattle driven over trail from Texas to Kansas named later for Jesse Chisholm.

1868 death of Jesse Chisholm

1873 retired Scots silk merchant George Grant imports Aberdeen Angus cattle to his Kansas colony

1876 Custer massacre at Battle of the Little Big Horn disrupts cattle drives from western Montana but leads to reservation life for Sioux

1878 Henry H 'Hank' Campbell impresses Chicago cattle packers with profits on Texas cattle. They invest in his Texas ranch

Europe	America
60% sent to Britain 1877-1879 Royal Commission on effects of imported beef and lamb show 30% profits that fuels Scottish investment in American West 1879	1880 thirty-three cattle companies floated in Scotland for Wild West ranching in
Prairie Land & Cattle Co. founded in Edinburgh to trade in Texas cattle. SS *Strathleven* carries first refridgerated US beef imports to England 1880 Dundee company incorporates HH Campbell's ranch as the Matador Land & Cattle Co. Highland crofters rent strikes copy Irish Land League to achieve full tenant rights 1882 1.1m cattle and 6.9m sheep in Scotland 1885 Liberal Government passes Crofting Act 1886 Buffalo Bill's Wild West Show winters in Glasgow as 700,000 attend performances 1891-92 wealthy American sportsman W Winnans rents 200,000 acres for exclusive shooting 1880 -95 250 deer forests in operation in Highlands. Falkirk Tryst replaced by local auction marts and rail freight from furthest Highlands, reaching Mallaig 1901 Buffalo Bill's Wild West and Congress of Rough Riders of the World tour Scottish towns reaching Inverness in Sept 1904 great international rodeo held at Wembley Stadium, London 1924 Scottish Parliament founded and abolished feudal land holding system 1999-2000	1880s RB Cunninghame Graham launches unsuccessful ranching projects in west Texas 1881 further foreign investment in US cattle fueled by James Brisbin's book Beef Bonanza 1883 peak droving year from Texas to Kansas railheads ships 350,000 cattle to eastern markets 1885 drought cuts cattle production. 5m cattle in Texas. Murdo MacKenzie hired by Prairie Co. to turn round profits 1886-87 winter Great Die Up kills half of cattle in West. Many cattle companies bankrupted. 1887 US law limits foreign ownership of land 1890 first Highland cattle exported to Canada; US cavalry massacre Sioux at Wounded Knee 1891 Murdo MacKenzie runs Matador Ranch 1892 Johnson County War, involves many Scottish ranchers v settlers 1900 South Dakota rancher Scotty Phillip buy small buffalo herd and saves the species 1910 Scotty Phillips dies 1917 Buffalo Bill dies 1929 Charlie Goodnight dies 1936 RB Cunninghame Graham dies in Buenos Aires and buried on Inchmahome, Scotland 1937 Murdo MacKenzie dies in Denver 1951 Matador Ranch sold to oil interests 1953 film *Shane* released 1956 John Ford's film *The Searchers* screened 1980 M Simino's film *Heavens Gate* released

Foreword

ROB GIBSON IS A HISTORIAN, folk music enthusiast and political campaigner with a passionate belief in Scots and Scotland. Yet he is well aware of Scotland in the wider world and the theme of the drover, the cowboy, the wandering Scot, brings all his many interests into play. *Plaids and Bandanas* began as a show featuring music, drama and slides, comparing the history of the Scottish cattle drover with that of the cattle trade in America, a trade that was significantly financed by Scottish capital and dependent on many colourful Scots. Just as another historian, Dr James Hunter, has chronicled the fascinating interaction between Scots and native North Americans, so has Rob Gibson now given the theme of cattle culture its rightful due. The show itself was a collage of sight and sound. Likewise this book is not dull history. Rather we learn of such characters as Corriecoillie, the irascible Highland drover, and Scots in America such as part-Cherokee Jesse Chisholm, or Murdo MacKenzie, John Clay and Scotty Philip – who helped save the American buffalo from extinction.

This small book has a large theme, well served by Gibson's obvious love for the picturesque or even eccentric. He also proves his ability to document main themes such as the effects of the cattle culture on the native peoples of both the Highlands and the western Plains. Rob Gibson has also long been a spokesman for land reform in Scotland and interesting parallels are drawn between land use and depletion in the American West and the Highlands.

This book, too, is an introduction to a greater theme: the Scot in the wider world, contributing to the history and culture of other nations through exploration, enterprise and adaptation. It is fitting then that *Plaids and Bandanas* has been performed in the Highlands and Lowlands but also in Canada and America. This reminds people thousands of miles from the great Highland drove roads that the ancient roots of Celtic cattle culture have survived into modern times, with all its danger, colour and flair.

Scots have long been aware of a Scottish diaspora that produced Indian chiefs, cowboys, gunslingers and outlaws. This fascinating study proves that the road from Dingwall to Falkirk extended as far as the Texas Panhandle and Alberta. As one whose own fortunes have taken him to Canada, America and back again, I would like to encourage readers of *Plaids and Bandanas* to go beyond Hollywood cliché and learn that the truth is even more colourful and fascinating. Plaid or bandana, the cattle trade was an international brotherhood and sisterhood whose story has now finally been explored with humour and sensitivity.

Tom Bryan

Introduction

CROICK CHURCHYARD, STRATHCARRON, in Easter Ross was for me this story's unlikely starting-point. I was being interviewed for a documentary, by Canadian filmmaker, Tom Radford charting the Scots and Irish roots of cowboy songs. The project's driving force, folk musician David Wilkie of Turner Valley, Alberta, had chanced on the words of a Gaelic cowboy song, *Mo Shoraidh Leis a' Coigich* – 'Leaving Coigach' – by Murdo MacLean. 'Surely there must be a lot more droving songs in Scotland?' he asked me on camera. My reply was hesitant. Only Brian McNeill's modern song, *Lads o the Fair,* came to mind:

> Come Geordie haud the pony
> For the way is steep and stony,
> Three lang weeks frae the Isle o Skye
> And the beasts are thin and bony,
> We'll take the last o the siller
> And we'll buy ourselves a gill or twa
> We'll drink tae the lads wha'll buy our kye
> In Falkirk Toon the morn.

I realised that, like most Scots, I probably knew more American cowboy songs than droving songs.

The old Parliamentary Church of Scotland at Croick contains poignant symbols of the clearance of eighteen Glencalvie families in May 1845. Slogans like 'Glencalvie people – the wicked generation, May 1845', and 'Blowship me to the colonies' have been scratched on the diamond-shaped panes of the east window of the church. Emigration from Scotland, whether forcible or voluntary, is one of the key threads in this story. It is also a thread linking David Wilkie, whose family hailed from West Lothian, and Rod Campbell, the man who first drew his attention to *Mo Shoraidh Leis a' Coigich*. Rod Campbell emigrated from Dingwall, Ross-shire, to settle in Edmonton, Alberta, in the 1970s. A folk music enthusiast, he heard of David's quest to find Scots and Irish links to cowboy music in 1995, and remembered seeing Murdo MacLean's song in a collection published to mark Ullapool's bi-centenary. *Ullapool: A Celebration in Music and Song* (1988) was compiled by Tom and Valerie Bryan, then raising their family in Strathkanaird. Valerie, a music teacher, met her Canadian-Scots husband-to-be in Sutherland and both attended a university in Indiana. Their decision to return to Scotland and put their energies into the old country's musical, social and cultural revival inspired Ullapool resident Andy Mitchell to write a song called *Indiana* which chronicled the Bryans' return to Scotland.[1]

Perhaps Scots have looked more to North America for music, films and culture than to our southern neighbours because of the scale of Scots emigration to the 'land of the free'. In my own family, my mother's father, Walter Rintoul, a ship's engineer from Leven in Fife, qualified at Poplar in the port of London in 1894 and worked on the refrigeration ships plying the South American beef trade to the UK. He tried to set up business in Brazil but failed and came back to London. There he met my grandmother, a civil servant from Fraserburgh. The couple returned to Scotland and for many years Walter worked for the Union Cold Storage Co. in George Street, Glasgow. As a reminiscence of his South American sojourn, their house in Brackenbrae Avenue, Bishopbriggs, was called Alameda. My mother's older sister Janet and her husband Johnny Myles also emigrated to the USA in the late 1920s.

On my father's side, some relatives went to Arizona at the turn of the century and family stories tell of armed Mexican raids on the settlements there. My uncle, Tom Gibson, visited the Arizona relatives in Phoenix in the 1950s and brought back gifts for us kids. I still possess a whole sheaf of *Arizona Highways* magazines from that era, full of extravagantly beautiful colour photography and Wild West history. But it was a pair of batwing chaps, the leather leggings which protect a rider from the thorny brush on the range, that gave me and my brother Iain a real prop for our childhood cowboy-and-indian games.

Little did I imagine then that this piece of cowboy apparel made for a five-foot high cowpuncher would end up being pressed into service for *Plaids and Bandanas*, the show Ceilidh Ménage launched at the 1998 Highland Festival. The chaps didn't fit my six-foot-plus frame but were just the trick for the petite Lizbeth Collie who paraded them to great effect in the cowboy section of our show. Our CD from *Plaids and Bandanas* was recorded in late 1998. During that time BBC Radio Scotland broadcast *Geronimo on Duke Street*, providing me with yet more links between Scotland and the Wild West. I discovered that in 1891, Buffalo Bill's Wild West Show had performed in the Exhibition Showground, not 200 yards from the house where I was brought up. American Indian performers had camped for three months in Glasgow's East End. At that time George Crager, Buffalo Bill's Indian interpreter, sold a Lakota Ghost Shirt and other artifacts to Glasgow's Kelvingrove Museum and Art Gallery. When the shirt was displayed in 1992 in the *Home of the Brave* exhibition, native Americans made the first moves to repatriate it. Eventually Glasgow Council agreed to send it to a museum in South Dakota. Guilt for the part played by Scots in these imperialist ventures sits uneasily with the oft-expressed solidarity of many individual Scots with the oppressed Sioux peoples. All this was played out in a heated debate at the time I began to explore drover-cowboy links.

The droving trade was well established in Scotland by the sixteenth century. In the Highlands of the seventeenth and eighteenth centuries, clanship was transformed into a very successful vehicle for commerce.[2] The clan gentry, close relations to the chiefs, provided the leadership. Chiefs-turned-landlords were to trigger profound changes in Highland society. They saw a switch to sheep ranching as a way to gain a six-fold increase in return over the rents obtained from cattle pastoralists. But sheep ranching could best be conducted in huge inland straths and hills once these were stripped of what incoming sheep-farmers like Patrick Sellar called 'the Aborigines' or 'these barbarous hordes'.

In North America, settlers encountered indigenous peoples whom they controlled, or exterminated, more completely than the Highlanders had been after Culloden. The actions of abused Scots as abusers of other native peoples in other continents have a familiar ring to the social psychologist. Unsurprisingly the mechanisms of 'improvement' already applied in Scotland were practiced even more ruthlessly in the New World. During the flood to 'modernise' the New World a remarkable number of Scots emigrants did sympathise with the native peoples and their ways of life, supporting their rights against the tide of corporate business.

> You came, you trapped, you charted,
> You laid the railroads and the schemes,
> And you tamed this land by enterprise
> And by the power of your dreams.[3]

This 'taming' of the American Frontier reached a peak between 1865 and 1890, a period that has been described as the Western Civil War of Incorporation.[4] There are uncanny parallels with the 'Highland Civil War of Subjugation' in the previous century.

I have organised the subject matter to lead on from the domestication of cattle in the Stone Age to the present world-wide cattle industry. The ancient Celts learned the skills of breeding, raiding and then trading cattle in an ever-expanding market. The long development of the international cattle trade between Scotland and England leads to the impact on Europe of stock production on the Western Plains of the USA, this being the culmination of a thousand years' development. The social importance of cattle on cultural life is traced through the same trajectory. The significance of key characters in the development of the cattle trade are assessed, as are the resultant pressures on indigenous peoples and land in both Scotland and the USA. Finally the impact of myths and realities are explored.

A chronology of events, glossary and indexed maps are provided to guide the reader as are sections on further reading, places of interest and musical recordings. While there are other source books on droving practice and many on cowboy skills, this book sets its focus on the striking range of economic, social, musical and personal experiences that link Celtic cattle culture and the cowboy life, particularly in the American West.

References

1. *Living Tradition,* issue 27, 1998 pp 22-23.
2. Allan I Macinnes, *Clanship, Commerce and the House of Stuart,* 1603-1788 (East Linton, Tuckwell Press, 1996).
3. From the Runrig song *Rocket to the Moon* from the album *Cutter and the Clan*, Ridge Records, 1987.
4. Clyde Milner et al, *The Oxford Book of the American West* (Oxford, OUP, 1974).

'Shuggy was expecting an Injun outfit, but noo we'll jist hiv tae play at Cowboys
an' Bus Conductors..'
(Cartoon from *Bud Neill's Magic!*, reproduced by permission of Zipo Publishing
with thanks to Ranald MacColl and the Neill family)

CHAPTER I

Cattle Breeders and Cattle Raiders

CATTLE WERE DOMESTICATED AT about the same time as Stone Age farmers settled in one place and grew their first primitive crops. The aurochs, the wild Eurasian bull that roamed the continent, was the ancestor of all modern cattle. It survived in the wild in Poland till the seventeenth century, but was first domesticated in Europe around 6000 BC. Breeds familiar today such as Highland cattle, Texas Longhorns or sleek, black Aberdeen Angus all derive from the great black aurochs and his smaller, reddish, female partner.

From around 8000 BC the last ice age receded and bit by bit broke up the extremities of the great north-western peninsula of Europe into the islands later named Ireland and Britain. Ice melted, land tilted, seas rose, and land bridges slowly sank while climatic changes eventually created the landscapes we recognise today. Wild mammals such as mammoths were isolated and wiped out on the islands and the remaining aurochs were gradually tamed. By around 2500 BC mixed oak forests, fields and grassland were common. Domesticated cattle reached Scotland and Ireland at this time in increasing numbers as settlers transported their valuable stock by primitive boats[1].

Windswept northern isles like Orkney relied on cattle for domestic consumption as excavations at Skara Brae on the Orkney Mainland reveal[2]. The community that lived there for over a thousand years produced sophisticated artefacts. They also left the bones of cattle, sheep, goats and pigs, fish and shellfish. Analysis of these bones show cattle and other livestock were much smaller than today's breeds, much as Shetland ponies still retain their tiny form today.

Stone Age people seemed to have prized the long-horned varieties of cattle although short-horned varieties were subsequently bred for easier management. Selecting cattle for their shape, colour and milking qualities was a skill passed down many generations as, from around 1200 BC, cattle culture successfully adapted to diverse habitats. Cattle farming took on increasing importance as cooler, wetter times brought about the formation of peat. This made it harder for Bronze Age farmers to grow and ripen corn in the wetter west and north.

By about 400 BC roving Celtic warbands from continental Europe used their iron swords and tools to impose their rule over most of the British Isles; like earlier communities, farming on landscapes of heather moor, pasture and forests of oak, beech and pine[3], these warlike Celts valued cattle as their main source of wealth. Cows were milked daily and their hides and meat used sparingly. Great numbers were given as dowries for princesses, showing that cattle had come to symbolise power and prosperity. According to bardic prophecy, successful Celtic kingships in Ireland and Scotland would be signalled by an abundance of milk from thriving cows.[4]

We learn more of the significance of cattle in Gaelic Ireland during early Celtic Christian times from the twelfth-century *Book of the Dun Cow*, a chronicle written by monks in the abbey of Clonmacnois, situated on the banks of the river Shannon, south of Athlone. The book itself was covered with the hides of the sacred dun cow. In it the monks made many references to Celtic cattle culture, in which the clan bards of old had celebrated in verse the warbands' prowess, raising cattle raiding to a heroic art form. The 'Cattle Raid of Cooley', *Tain*

Bo Cuailnge, was written down by the monks of Clonmacnois from what is thought to be the oldest vernacular epic poem in Western Europe. Its oral roots date from around the first centuries after the birth of Christ when Ireland was still pagan. It tells of Finnbennach a white-horned bull owned by Aillil, king of Connaught. Aillil's wife Medb was jealous so she tried to buy the brown bull of Cuailgne, Donn Cuailgne, from Daire mac Fiachnai in Ulster. He refused and brought invasion on his country by the men of Connaught and its defence by the Hound of Ulster, Cuchulain.

Thomas Kinsella's translation of the *Tain* into English gives us a taste of the naturalistic vigour of the original. The two bulls at the story's heart are described below:

> This was the Brown Bull of Cuailgne –
> dark brown dire haughty with young health
> horrific overwhelming ferocious
> full of craft
> furious fiery flanks narrow
> brave brutal thick breasted
> curly browed head cocked high
> growling and eyes glaring
> tough maned neck thick and strong
> snorting mighty in muzzle and eye
> with a true bull's brow
> and a wave's charge
> and a royal wrath
> and the rush of a bear
> and a beast's rage
> and a bandit's stab
> and a lion's fury.

Thirty grown boys could take
their place from rump to nape
– a hero to his herd at morning
foolhardy at the herd's head
to his cows the beloved
to the husbandman a prop
the father of great beasts
overlooks the ox of the earth.

A white head and white feet
had the bull Finnbennach
and a red body the colour of blood
as if bathed in blood
or dyed in the red bog
or pounded in purple
with its blank paps
under breast and back
and his heavy mane and great hoofs
the beloved of the cows or Ai
with ponderous tail
and a stallion's breast
and a cow's eye apple
and a salmon's snout
and hinder haunch
he romps in rut
born to bear victory
bellowing in greatness
idol of the ox herd
the prime demon Finnbennach.[5]

For every cattle breeder there was an envious cattle-raider tempted to increase the clan's wealth, so that long-distance cattle theft became endemic in Ireland and Scotland. A ritual cattle raid, or *creach*, in Scots Gaelic, was an accepted custom of the country. Celtic clan chiefs required little reason for such raids beyond the potential prestige and they served as a rite of passage for young chiefs. *Spreidh* is the Scots Gaelic for a freelance raid or one of the many forays made over the centuries by Highland Scots in search of cattle on the lands of their richer Lowland neighbours.

We know of one such *spreidh* that took place in 600 AD when the lands around the Solway Firth were ruled by King Urien of Rheged, a Welsh-speaking Celtic warlord, whose bard bragged, 'when he returned in the autumn from the country of the men of the Clyde, no cow lowed to her calf'.[6] Urien's victims and booty came from the neighbouring Welsh-speaking kingdom Strathclyde, to the north of Rheged.

Cattle raiding was woven into the very fabric of national life. Just like the Highlanders, Border families led a predominantly pastoral life, and raided each others' hills and dales; with the centuries-old enmity between Scotland and England, it was often seen as legitimate to capture as much of your enemy's moveable assets as possible. The deeds of Border reivers, as these cattle raiders were called, became the stuff of countless ballads. Generally, raids took place in the autumn when crops were harvested and cattle in prime condition.

One of the earliest surviving Border Ballads tells of the Battle of Otterburn in 1388. The opening stanza pinpoints the time of year and emphasises the object of driving off English cattle:

It fell about the Lammas tide,
When the muir men win their hay,
The doughty Douglas bound him to ride
Into England to drive a prey.

This raid on Northumberland reached as far as the gates of Newcastle, the stronghold of the Percy earls, where challenges were uttered and much booty and livestock driven off. Though the Scots leader, the Earl of Douglas, was slain on the return journey, his men managed to keep his death a secret and won the day.

Further north, in 1392, a host of clansmen led by a grandson of King Robert II, who was known as the Wolf of Badenoch, raided out of the Highlands into the Braes of Angus and Stormont in Perthshire. This culminated in a pitched battle with angry locals at the castle of Glascune near Blairgowrie as the raiders were driving off the cattle from Angus farms. Similar events, if not on such a grand scale, were a common occurrence till long after the Union of the Crowns in 1603.

In the century after 1493 when the Lordship of the Isles was finally forfeit by James IV, King of Scots, the Highlands and Islands lost all political stability, which led to a great increase in organised cattle raiding. For example, in the southern Highlands the MacGregors, of the Trossachs east of Loch Lomond, and their neighbours, the MacFarlanes of Arrochar and Inveruglas to the west of the loch, co-operated in reselling stolen cattle. Each clan had its favoured raiding places. With speed and stealth the MacGregors struck out east among the farms of Strathearn whilst the MacFarlanes struck the Cowal peninsula on the Clyde coast. Following these raids they met at the appointed spot to swap beasts for onward sale to unsuspecting clients.

Appropriately the MacFarlanes boasted as a clan pipe tune

Thogail nam Bo – 'Lifting the Cattle'. The song boasted of driving off cattle through high passes between the glens. These feats of endurance were achieved in autumn sleet and rain. Sometimes the cattle were driven away past the first frozen lochs of early winter and through drifting snows. These stealthy skills might reap but little financial reward, yet they were a matter of pride among communities whose scarce means were eked out by daring cattle theft.

Clans such as the Farquharsons of Deeside and the MacGregors of the Trossachs derived additional income from protection money known as 'black mail'. 'Mail' or 'meal' derives from the old Scots word for rent. This black rent was extorted from their Lowland neighbours in return for pledges not to steal livestock and to guard the adjacent hill passes against other potential raiders; black mail was therefore an extra source of income in the cattle-lifting business.

The ballad *The Baron o Brackley* merges two 'cattle battles' in 1592 and 1666 into one story. Enmity between two families in Upper Deeside carried on through generations. An argument had been simmering between John Gordon of Brackley and Farquharson of Inverey over an impounded herd of cattle, or kye. His faithless wife goaded Brackley to protect their herd:

> Oh rise up my baron and turn back your kye,
> For the lads fae Drumwharran are a driving them by

Her husband replied:

> Oh how can I rise up and turn them again
> For whaur I hae aye man, I'm sure they hae ten

Finally rising to his scheming wife's taunts, Brackley rode out, but as he predicted:

> There cam' wi' fause Inverey thirty and three,

There was nane wie bonny Brackley but his brother and he,
Twa gallanter Gordons did never sword draw,
But against three and thirty, wae is me what is twa?

The treachery of Brackley's widow was revealed when she feasted with Inverey and the seeds were sown of another deadly feud:

There's grief in the kitchen but there's mirth in the ha'
For the Baron o' Brackley is deid and awa'
But up spoke his son on the nurse's knee
'Gin I live tae be a man revenged I'll be.

During the late sixteenth century, a very active cattle reiver called Wat o Harden lived near Hawick in the Scottish Borders. It is said that his wife served his spurs on a dinner plate whenever she wanted to remind him that stocks of beef were low and that it was time to mount a new cattle raid. Such was the pragmatic attitude of Border Scots towards cattle lifting.

Cattle raiding reduced considerably along the Border as King James VI of Scots became James I of England in 1603 and trade opened up. Further north, troops were garrisoned in the Highlands. By the 1650s they were reinforced at the south end of the Great Glen, and by 1690 at Fort William. But some years before that, in 1670, Martin Martin, the traveller and writer, mentions the last recorded *creach* taking place. In *A Description of the Western Isles* he cites Angus Macdonald of Achluachrach, scion of the Keppoch sept, celebrating his impending marriage by making a predatory raid with twelve associates into the estates of the Roses of Kilravock in Nairnshire. In a high-speed operation, the MacDonald raiders dodged the soldiers and irate pursuit from the Nairn men. They thought nothing of a 250-mile round trip from the Rough

Bounds in the west Highlands right across hill and glen to raid the lush east coast farms and back again.

Cattle raids didn't end till much later in the eighteenth century though they were made more difficult after General Wade's military road-building programme, which was designed to speed the journeys of government troops to any trouble spot. Captain Edward Burt, an English Hanoverian army officer who was stationed in the Highlands around 1730 as a road surveyor, despised the expression 'cattle lifting'. His reminiscences, *Letters from a Gentleman in the North of Scotland* (1754) show his contempt:

> The stealing of cows they call lifting, a softening word for theft, as if it were only collecting their dues.... the principal time for this wicked practice is the Michaelmas moon when the cattle are in condition fit for market... if the pursuers overtake the robbers and find them inferior in numbers and happen to seize any of them, they are seldom prosecuted, there being few who are in circumstances fit to support the expense of a prosecution...

A *spreidh* came to grief at Strathmore, Lochbroom in Wester Ross when Lochaber raiders, resting beside their captured herd near Braemore, killed and roasted a beast. But their celebrations were short-lived for the pursuers led by MacMurchaidh Riabhaich surprised them and slew all the raiders to a man except for the watchman, who was sent home with the gory news. This incident appears to have occurred around 1746, making the Braemore *spreidh* one of the last.

With the advent of an increasingly peaceful and commercial climate in Hanoverian Britain, the demand for beef soared in the prosperous towns of England and Scotland. This required longer and bigger droves posing more opportunities for cattle rustling and black mail. In the general disorder following the last Jacobite rising in 1745-46, Graham of Gartmore in Stirlingshire calculated that £37,000 was lost from cattle theft to stockmen and lairds in and around the edges of the Highlands.

The Celts bred hardy beasts and skilled drovers, many of whom honed their skills in the heat of a *spreidh*. Some idea of that age-old way of life is of interest before looking at the drovers and their skills.

References

1. Ian Grimble, *Highland Man* (Inverness, HIDB, 1980), p 14.
2. AT Lucas, *Cattle in Ancient Ireland* (Kilkenny, Bothius Press, 1989), p 13.
3. Fergus Kelly, *Early Irish Farming* (Institute for Advanced Studies, Dublin, 1999), pp 35-36.
4. Thomas Kinsella, trans., *The Tain* (Portlaoise, Dolmen Press, 1969), pp 49-50.
5. Allan I Macinnes, *Clanship, Commerce and the House of Stuart*, 1603-1788 (East Linton, Tuckwell Press, 1996), pp 33.
6. Quoted by WJ Watson, *The Celtic Place-Names of Scotland* (Edinburgh, Birlinn, 1998 reprint), p 156.

CHAPTER 2

Cattle Culture and the Sheiling Life

HIGHLAND LIVES WERE DOMINATED for centuries by the seasonal rhythms of cattle rearing. This includes the summer sheiling system that has left so many references in poem and song. In Gaelic *bo* is a cow, *tarbh* a bull, *crodh* a cattle herd or dowry. In the Lowlands cattle are *kye* and in Caithness and Sutherland English *kyloes*. The economy was underpinned by the remarkable efficiency of their cattle rearing practices. As pioneering eco-scientist Frank Fraser Darling noted in *West Highland Survey*:

> ... the old-time cattle breeding husbandry of the Highlands and Islands was so well organised it might have been planned on the basis of a policy, but we know that it grew and merely became trimmed to its definite system by time and circumstance.[1]

A damp climate and rough terrain in much of Scotland made pastoral agriculture essential for survival. Unlike present-day commercial cattle breeds, black cattle took three or four summers to mature so only the strongest cattle survived the cold, wet winters and a very hardy strain of beasts evolved. Poverty and a lack of hay didn't daunt Highland farmers; in summer their practice of taking cattle to fresh pastures at hill sheilings continued until the mid-nineteenth century. In the autumn, unsold beasts were identified as those for slaughter and those for salting down for winter supplies. Of the rest only the strongest survived. In the winter the beasts might share the family's own roof, often in a lightly partitioned section next to the living space of the typical

Highland black house. The cattle offered extra heat in the cold weather. Others were over-wintered in woodland that provided shelter and some extra food from the tree bark and dead grass.

Haymaking was uncertain so in most of the wetter west it was not practised till modern times. Only in the south of Ireland was year-round growth of grass expected, while in northern Scotland winter food shortages occurred regularly. That is why emergency cattle food such as holly and ivy had to be sought. Early Irish texts mention the use of holly and ivy as emergency fodder. Holly is native to most parts except Caithness, Orkney and Shetland, so its use would have been widespread. One of the Celts' seven 'noble trees of the forest', holly was also prized for its hard, white wood and made excellent spits for roasting meat. The Gaelic, Welsh and Anglo-Saxon names for holly are, respectively, *cuileann, celyn* and *holen,* and would appear to be closely related. Cross-border drovers would often stop at drove stances in the north of England the place-names of which had the prefix 'hollin', e.g. Hollinshead. This prefix suggests that a similar longstanding solution in face of hardship was widespread throughout the British Isles.[2]

Driving of cattle to hill pastures allowed winter dung to be spread on the in-bye run-rigs where bere, a primitive form of barley, was sown, safe from ravenous ponies, sheep and cattle. Technically called transhumance, this practice both protected the crops near the baile or village and made the most of new growth on summer hill grazings. Each year the women and children would drive the beasts many miles to summer sheilings, camping under rough shelters to herd the cattle in hill corries.

The Highland sheiling system lasted into the early nineteenth century. According to legend, Brigit, the patron saint of cattle and herding, was nurtured as a child from the milk of a white, red-eared cow. In his evidence to the 1883 Napier Commission on Crofting, Alexander Carmichael, the folk tale collector, quoted a South Uist Gaelic blessing, *The Herding Rune*:

Travel ye moorland, travel ye townland
Travel ye gently far and wide
God's son be the herdsman about your feet
Whole may ye home return
The protection of God and Columba
Encompass your going and coming
And about you be the milkmaid
With the smooth white palms
Bridget of the clustering hair, golden brown.

The summer sheiling pastures helped produce milk, curds, cream, butter and cheese before the killing of cattle for meat took place as a winter contingency. For the young people, summer meant exhilarating freedom from the close confines of the black house. The chroniclers of St Columba of Iona alleged that he would caution his monks, 'Where a cow is, a woman will be; where a woman is, temptation will be.'

Bards like Rob Donn MacKay often celebrated sheiling life in song and verse. Born in 1714 in Strathnaver, he practised his widely acclaimed, bardic skills well into the 1770s, entertaining people at all levels of clan society in north Sutherland with his satires, elegies and love songs. His life coincided with a halcyon period for the MacKays who were Hanoverian supporters in an area of Scotland remote from political upheaval. In later life, he stopped composing. By that time a new emphasis on estate management involved the fashionable theory that gaining maximum profit was imperative. The earlier, easy-going cattle culture was seen as an impediment to progress. Estate trustees were employed to manage the affairs of the Earl of Sutherland and the MacKays of Bighouse, both land-owning families having been afflicted by a series of untimely deaths that led to under-age inheritances.

Rob Donn's poems were passed on by word of mouth during his lifetime and were only written down latterly. As a drover's lad he herded cattle from the MacKay country, notably from the grazings near his Strathmore home. As part of the larger MacKay droves he visited Crieff Cattle Tryst many times. Like future cowboys in the American West he dreamt of being back with his sweetheart in the 'little glen of the calves' rather than to be counting the cattle in the parks of Crieff. In the romantic tradition, he returned to find his youthful dreams shattered and he laments, a little tongue in cheek, that he would be the better for a kiss from her, before leaving the country.[3]

Rob Donn's verse memorialised a way of life that was passing after thousands of years. Songs of this sort would be carried across the oceans and transformed by word of mouth wherever lonely drovers, miners and loggers felt the pangs of homesickness. For the Celtic cattle culture meant far more than just tending the herds.

References
1. Frank Fraser Darling, *West Highland Survey* (Oxford, OUP, 1955), p 239.
2. MA Atkin, 'Hollin Names in North-West England', *Nomina, a journal of name studies, relating to Great Britain and Ireland*, Vol XII 1988-9.
3. Ian Grimble, *The World of Rob Donn* (Edinburgh, Saltire Society, 1999), pp 18 and 22.

CHAPTER 3

Highland Cattle – a Breed Evolves

HOW DO TODAY'S CATTLE compare with the cattle of ancient Celtic Scotland, Ireland and Wales, for size, docility, colour, milking qualities and meat? Experts agree that the size and build of modern Kerry cattle are a good measure of ancient Celtic cattle. Present day Dexters, Shetland cattle and Welsh Blacks are all, by size and temperament, a good comparison.

There is graphic evidence from around twenty Pictish sculptured stones around Scotland. These show in stylised images that polled (hornless) and horned cattle were widely revered in the lands of the Picts and the Scots in the early Middle Ages. These were the forebears of the cattle that would provide the sires and dams for nineteenth-century scientific breeders. It appears that Picts at Burghead in Morayshire practised bull worship. Perhaps to appease their Celtic water spirits, stones engraved with polled bulls appear to have been thrown into the bay below the great fort. Many were found when the local harbour was first dredged and deepened in the nineteenth century. Folklore concerning bull sacrifices in the Moray area was recorded in the eighteenth century. It seems that Pictish pagan ideas lasted long after the Picts were absorbed into the Scottish kingdom.

The utility of early cattle was shown in 1963 in an experiment carried out with the rare Dexter breed by the Ancient Fields Research Committee of the Council of British Archaeology. At one of the Council's evening classes the tutor was describing the ancient Celtic cattle, when one student,

Lettice Dawson, announced, 'I have one just like that at home'. Mrs Dawson and her husband Jock agreed to train their Dexters to pull a plough made of oak and birch, such as the Celts would probably have used. The wooden plough turned the soil on the chalk down lands of south-east England in preparation for sowing seed. This experiment confirmed that the breed was suitable not only for milking and meat but also for working the land, just as their Celtic cattle ancestors had been.[1]

The significance of cattle in everyday life is indicated in the number of times they are mentioned in wills and bequests. These include both horned and polled Black Highland cattle. For instance a will written in 1523 in favour of John Comyn of Culter, Aberdeenshire, instructed him to take possession of his deceased father's estate by accepting a black polled bullock or plough ox, symbolising his right to cultivate the ground.[2]

Smaller types of cattle were far more manageable on a drove than the larger breeds of today would be. At the end of the eighteenth century the carcass of a four-year-old kylo would be 360 to 400 lbs; if fattened in England, up to 560 lbs could be achieved. 'The price is generally according to the size and shape but occasionally varies according to demand'.[3] As science developed in the nineteenth century, a 30 to 40 per cent increase in weight was achieved and the characteristics of modern beef and milk breeds established.

In the early eighteenth century Irish cattle were imported to south-west Scotland for breeding purposes, despite the ban on Irish imports imposed in 1667. However, by the end of the century English and Galloway stock were being introduced into north-east Ireland to improve the stock there. Mr Fullarton of Ayr suggests this turnaround was due to the lower prices paid by dealers in Scotland and England for Irish cattle that 'were wide horned and raw boned, so difficult to fatten.' At a price of £2 to £3 they were cheaper than Ayrshires, but inferior in quality.

In the second quarter of the eighteenth century, the spirit of improvement was spreading. The Duke of Argyll embarked on major agricultural and industrial improvements.[4] Campbell of Knockbuy, Minard on Loch Fyneside boasting of his enclosures and stockbreeding experiments in 1744 commented:

> ... the Galloway gentlemen acknowledge these several years past my cattle were inferior to no Highlanders grazed with them; which demonstrates Argyllshire is as capable as Galloway for that purpose, though the latter has run away with the profit for many years back, which proper attention and application might alwise preserve to the Shire of Argyll.

In the 1790s another prominent agricultural improver, Sir John Sinclair of Ulbster, Caithness, commissioned the first statistical account to be compiled by Scottish ministers to detail the life of their parishes. In his review of their efforts, published in 1831, he concluded that Black Cattle were being selectively improved: 'The Scotch breed of cattle are of a superior description. No stock sold better to the English markets, or is more relished at table.' Although cattle were selected for various qualities from time to time, the ancient types of cattle raised in many localities of pastoral Scotland for two thousand years would indeed form the basis for scientific breeding. But Scots cattle cannot be called a 'breed' as such before the mid-nineteenth century.

Some far-sighted drovers became cattle breeders, especially in the counties of north-east Scotland where winter feed crops like hay and turnips, introduced in the eighteenth century, made this possible. In the early 1800s Hugh Watson of Keilor in Angus and Robert Walker at West Fintray, Aberdeenshire crossed black, polled cattle (called, in local dialect, doddies or humbies) with West Highlanders bought for them by local cattle dealers, the Williamson brothers, from their usual sources in the Highland glens.

Major English breeding trials begun in the 1740s used the enclosures and agricultural improvements introduced in Norfolk. Such ideas, central to the Agricultural Revolution, spread within decades to the north of Scotland. Nevertheless the native Black Cattle were in high demand until the mid-nineteenth century. Such were the cattle bought from Islay at the local trysts in May or June. Drovers would ferry them across to Jura, drive on half-way up the east coast to Lagg and from there ferry the herds to the mainland at Keills at the mouth of loch Sween on mainland Argyll. After being fattened on mainland pasture the beasts were driven to the Falkirk Tryst in September.

The dominant hues of these distinctive beasts ranged between black, reddish brown and tan. Selective breeding increased colour diversity and brindled, dun, brown, yellow and red cattle became more common. As noted by historian John Prebble and others, the black cattle described by early nineteenth-century agriculturalists included the red and red-brown animals so frequently portrayed by mid-century landscape artists.

In 1802 one of the Stewarts of Glenlyon shipped selected red cattle to the Hebrides to form the first improved herd, or fold of the Highland breed. The distinctive red colour, good milking qualities, hardiness, docility and increased size were the outstanding features of this new strain of Highland Cattle.[5]

With the spread north of the railway network and the introduction of regular steamship services to south-east England, the north-east of Scotland gained particular advantage in marketing its much-improved animals. Cattle breeder William McCombie used these routes to take stock south, and in 1868 he went on to win a Smithfield prize. These new modes of transport effectively marked the end of the days of the great droves from the Highlands.

An old drover, Dugald MacDougall of Argyllshire, remarked in the 1950s 'when they got... into fancy things, they did away with the black ones. There's hardly any left of the black cattle.'[6] The gingery, shaggy, long-horned Highland breed of today has become a symbol of the north-west of Scotland's place in our cattle-breeding heritage, instead of small, black cattle.

The great cattle-rearing areas in the world were to experiment with various breeds to strengthen their stock. In 1881 the XIT Ranche Co. in Texas imported Aberdeen Angus bloodstock. In 1890 Lord Strathcarron exported a West Highland bull and twenty females of the Highland breed to Canada to establish the breed in the New World. Although it was found by trial and error that Hereford cattle were more suited to conditions on the Great Plains of Texas and the south-west, the Scots breeds were nevertheless important contributors to stock rearing, from the pampas of Argentina to the northern pastures of Wyoming, Montana and Alberta.

References

1. *Book of the Dexter*, p 27.

2. Barclay and Keith, *A History of the Aberdeen-Angus Breed*, (Aberdeen 1958).

3. James MacDonald, *A General View of Agriculture in the Hebrides* (1811).

4. LE Cochran, *Scots Trade with Ireland in the 18th Century* (Edinburgh, John Donald, 1985).

5. T. McLatchie, *A Brief History of Highland Cattle* (printed in the Oban Times, 1991). Copy supplied by the Highland Cattle Society.

6. Dugald MacDougall interviewed by Eric Cregeen, 'Recollections of an Argyllshire Drover' (*Scottish Studies*, 3, 1959), p 148.

The far-famed Aberdeen Angus breed

In the 1740s, Campbell of Knockbuy reached the conclusion that experiments to cross native Highland cattle with Galloway cattle and other breeds produced inferior stock. Before the Aberdeen Angus breed was successfully established, English dealers still preferred the West Highland black cattle. In *A General View of the Agriculture of the County of Argyll* (1805) Dr John Smith warned that, 'crossing the true Highland breed with any other ought to be avoided... the native cattle are always the hardiest cattle and the best feeders.'

It was a systematic breeding programme begun around 1810 by Hugh Watson of Keilor in Angus that was consolidated by William McCombie of Tillyfour, Aberdeenshire. McCombie (1805-80) can be called the master builder of the Aberdeen Angus breed. He had been critical of the cross-breeding of native cattle with southern breeds that he considered inferior and far less hardy. This guided McCombie and Watson who both favoured black dodded cattle as the basis of their breed trials. McCombie later described his breed as a 'utilitarian choice that was easier to handle, hardy unlike the English shorthorns and economical to feed.' The qualitative improvements they brought about were a 30 to 40 percent increase in size over a forty-year period including the much-prized marled texture of the butcher meat. Improved feed based on growing drilled turnips as a staple feed crop along with clover pastures in enclosed fields was a major advance for over-wintering healthy stock. This coincided with the introduction of horses and the reduced use of oxen as motive power on improved farms. Nevertheless it took William McCombie till 1868 for his own Aberdeen Angus to sweep the boards at the prestigious Smithfield Show in London.

The Aberdeen Angus breed had already become a major contributor to both pure and cross-bred stock in worldwide prime beef production. By 1860 Aberdeen Angus cattle had been presented by Lord South Esk to SMG Simpson and exported to Canada for duties on the Canadian and United States plains. George Grant, a retired silk merchant from Morayshire, who established an extravagant colony on the Kansas Prairies, imported Aberdeen Angus cattle in 1873. Many other ranchers across the globe were to build their quality herds from Aberdeen Angus stock.

CHAPTER 4

A Huge Droving Trade Evolves

THE GREAT SKILL OF the *creach* and *spreidh* was to drive herds of cattle, horses and sheep speedily and safely through trackless glens and over hill passes in all weathers. The commercial droving trade was built on these skills.

In the seventeenth century most of Scotland's surplus beef was still sold at local fairs, with a few of the strongest beasts kept for breeding purposes over winter. However, there had been an international trade as early as the fourteenth century. We know from the Foedera Records[1] that in 1359 Andrew Moray and Alan Erskine, plus three horsemen and servants, were granted safe conduct to travel through England for one year to prosecute their sale of Scottish cattle and horses. (This was towards the end of the Scottish Wars of Independence, warfare that had dragged on for over sixty years following the death of Alexander III in 1286). The likely source of these cattle for cross-border trade was Galloway, an autonomous south-west province with its own laws. We know of cattle being exported from the Isle of Skye to Inverness in 1502 and, by implication, further south. This indicates the widespread development of droving in both south-west and northern Scotland.

During the seventeenth century, traditional cattle markets in larger royal burghs like Edinburgh, Glasgow and Aberdeen were augmented by further business derived from growing burghs like Dundee, Perth and Stirling. As the century advanced and in response to the growing demands of London, the Scottish droving trade took increasing numbers of cattle south in marathon six-week journeys.

Families from all levels in society specialised in droving. In the early 1720s, in the MacKay lands of Durness, Strathmore and Strath Halladale, two of the leading gentry, Iain MacEachainn of Muisel, third cousin of Lord Reay, and the chief's son Hugh MacKay of Big House, took charge of the cattle trade and of the deer hunts in the MacKay lands. About a century after their Lowland counterparts, Highland lairds were also turning themselves into landed proprietors. By acquiring title deeds after the Reformation in 1560, Lowland lairds had already shared out kirk lands and secularised estates. This was the precursor to the early agricultural improving movement that was to flower in the eighteenth century.

Professor Allan Macinnes's *Clanship, Commerce and the House of Stewart* points to evidence of increased feudal conveyancing in Argyllshire where the number on the register of heritors or tax payers increased from 265 in 1629 to 337 by 1688. As warfare reduced, commerce increased. The minor clan gentry were able to underwrite their chiefs' lavish lifestyles through wadsets, or mortgages, provided by droving profits. In the last two decades of the seventeenth century the gentry of droving clans had to conduct an annual search for letters of credit from Edinburgh goldsmiths and merchants before seeking to buy stock. This required character references from at least two major landowners.

Would-be drovers had to grapple with tight credit conditions. Potential backers were highly cautious because the ups and downs of the droving trade were notorious. These conditions were eased by the foundation in 1723 of Coutts & Company, a private bank, and of the Royal Bank of Scotland in 1727, breaking the monopoly that the ultra-conservative Bank of Scotland had held for thirty years. This release of credit enabled substantial loans to drovers to be agreed. In 1767 the British

Linen Bank made advances of £500 each to two Scottish drovers and £2,000 to a well-known Yorkshire drover.

Drovers would range to the farthest glens and islands gathering stock, but the cattle-rearing families in those parts received very little cash. Usually payment was in bills of credit that became a new form of money. The drovers had few scruples about paying as little as possible even though the clansmen relied on cattle sales to pay their rents. The success of this system of credit acted as a model that encouraged other forms of commerce in the industrial revolution such as textile manufacture. Inevitably bankruptcies occurred and complaints arose about the system's instability. But the strength of the credit system lay in the fact that it was based on well-informed character references.

Rob Roy MacGregor was a master drover. He was born in March 1671, the third son of Donald Glas, a chief of the Clan Gregor of Glengyle at the head of Loch Katrine. As a lad he accompanied his father to Edinburgh each spring to find financial backers for the business.[2] But many years of success as a drover came to an end in 1712 through the alleged arrears of £1,000 stake money. His chief drover, MacDonald of Monachyle Tuarach, apparently absconded, instead of buying cattle. This led to Rob's bankruptcy and a deadly feud with his former business backer, the Marquis of Montrose. It meant that Rob's family was forced to lead a hunted existence, his outlaw status compounded by his well-known Jacobite sympathies, and only eased in his last years. The recent discovery and sale of a letter dated 1724 uniquely signed 'Ro: Roy', not the usual 'Robert Campbell', indicates his continued practice of extracting black mail to keep the tenant farmers' cattle safe. He calls on Montrose's factor, Buchanan to meet him and pay a sum of money 'if yow have a mind that we will concerne with the Keeping of country'. He died ten years later and well within a century he was to become the plaything of Walter Scott's romantic pen.

In the two decades before the '45 Rising, Archibald Campbell, 2nd laird of Knockbuy, Argyll, conducted a very successful droving partnership with his kinsman, Campbell of Inverawe, sometimes moving as many as 2,000 cattle in the year. Their beasts were purchased on the islands of Islay, Jura and Mull, and from the West Highland mainland as far north as Moidart. The cattle were grazed on the parks at Knockbuy until they were ready to be driven to the Lowland trysts.[3]

After Culloden the Duke of Cumberland, 'The Butcher', opted for a scorched earth policy. In May 1746 new headquarters were established at Fort Augustus from which communities in Glenelg, Kintail, Lochaber and Morvern were pillaged and torched. Fort Augustus, supplied by the booty plundered from the population of the surrounding districts, became for a time the largest cattle market in Scotland. It was reckoned that in one year alone nearly 20,000 head of cattle were put up for sale, as well as numerous sheep, oxen, horses and goats.[4]

The military involvement in the cattle trade favoured Hanoverian supporters like the Frasers of Stratherrick and the MacKays of north-west Sutherland. Meanwhile English drovers who used to attend fairs of cattle in the borders of the north at Crieff and Doune, now had to go into the heart of the country[5], something that became much easier as Wade's military road network spread to the west coast.

The market price of a three or four-year-old cow increased from around £1.7s in 1707 to around £4 by the end of the century by which time it cost 7s 6d to drive each beast from Caithness to Carlisle, with an additional £1 expense to get to the Norfolk markets.

Many a barefoot Highland lad learned his trade on the road

to Crieff and Falkirk, taking home news of the outside world, its politics, styles, sights and sounds. But the mutual respect between clansfolk and clan chiefs weakened as the eighteenth century progressed.

In 1773 some tenants of Lord Reay of the Earldom of Sutherland embarked on the emigrant ship *Bachelor* to journey to the Carolinas. They were shipwrecked off Shetland and the records of the harbour authorities reveal their reasons for emigrating. Twenty-six-year-old William MacKay from Craigie is quoted as saying that:

> the rent of his possession was raised to double at the same time as the price of cattle was reduced one half, and even lower as he was obliged to sell them to the factor at what price he pleased.

Factors for MacKay of Big House had been extracting revenue to meet the laird's burden of debt. In addition, most of this party of emigrants came from the estates of the young Countess of Sutherland. Her trustees had also been forcing up estate revenue. Hugh Matheson of Kildonan mentioned that his rent had been more than doubled and:

> the price of cattle has been so low of late, and that of bread so high, that the factor, who was also a drover, would give no more than a boll of meal for a cow and obliged the tenants to give him their cattle at his own price.

The official retribution following Culloden in 1746 included the banning of tartan, weapons and bagpipes. This played a big part in the end of clanship but it was the determination of the chiefs-turned-lairds to maximise rents that destroyed first the livelihood of the tacksman class, then the commons of the clans. The Disarming Acts, notably, exempted drovers.

Former Jacobite Highlanders who became British soldiers cemented their loyalty to the Hanoverian dynasty by giving service against the French in North America. The soldiers were often demobbed there, drawing further emigrants from among their families and neighbours.

Throughout the eighteenth century trade in cattle, kelp, timber, charcoal, seasonal work in the Lowlands and illicit whisky production added to the Highland economy. However, cattle seem to have been the most profitable commodity of all until about the middle of the eighteenth century. Textiles, whisky and sheep had pushed the value of cattle exports into fourth or fifth place by 1800, despite the expansion in the cattle trade.

I agree with historian Bruce Lenman's rejection of the fashionable eighteenth century idea, which prevailed well into the nineteenth-century, that the Highlander was savage and his economy primitive. 'The first epithet is little better than a lie, while the second is at best gross over-simplification'[6]

The rash adventure of Prince Charles Edward Stuart's French-backed, failed rising in 1745 brought in its wake indiscriminate repression, the destruction and break-up of townships, and wholesale 'improvements' which were the Whig prescription for the country. This hastened the end of the age-old cattle culture, the clearance of the commons of the clans and the introduction of the Cheviot sheep. In order to understand the evolution of clanship into the age of commerce we need to reflect in more detail on what was so ruthlessly transformed.

References

1. Rhymer, Foedera, *Records Commission* (Edinburgh 1825), III part 1, p 415.
2. Ian Grimble, *The World of Rob Donn* (Edinburgh, Saltire Society, 1979 and 1999).

3. W.H. Murray, *Rob Roy MacGregor: His Life and Times* (Edinburgh, Canongate, 1982 & 1993), particularly chapters 6 & 13.

4. Cregeen, p 145.

5. TM Devine, *The Scottish Nation 1700-2000* (London, Allen Lane, 1999), p 46.

6. AJ Youngson, *After the '45* (Edinburgh, Edinburgh University Press, 1973), p 211.

7. Bruce Lenman, *An Economic History of Modern Scotland* (London, Batsford, 1977), p 87.

Scott's tale of two drovers

Written in 1827 in the heyday of cattle droving and at the height of Sir Walter Scott's fame, 'The Twa Drovers' was published in a collection entitled *Chronicles of the Canongate*. The story captures the colour of the Doune Tryst and portrays latent rivalry between Highland gentleman Robin Oig McCombich, or MacGregor, and an English yeoman Harry Wakefield as they drive their cattle on to market in England. A quarrel over grazing rights escalates into a violent double tragedy. Scott compares Robin's exaggerated Highland sense of honour to that of the Cherokee Indians. This tale takes a distinctly superior Lowland perspective, yet it is free of the romantic atmospherics that are the hallmark of his major novel, *Rob Roy*. 'The Twa Drovers' is a keenly observed picture of the realities of droving life.

CHAPTER 5

Better to Sell Nowte than Nations

SEVERAL OUTBREAKS OF THE Black Death occurred in Europe in the mid-fourteenth-century. These killed around a third of the human population. An increase in animal husbandry ensued because it was less labour intensive than crop growing. Consequently numbers of sheep and cattle increased as pastoral agriculture grew in importance. Demand for wool and meat eventually revived and an export trade commenced, interrupted in times of want when the Scottish authorities forbade the export of sheep, cattle and grain, as the Scottish Exchequer Rolls show. Nevertheless 45,000 hides were exported in 1378. Most of these would have been cattle hides, although some may have been deer skins.

Tensions between Scotland and England flared up at various points. In 1544 Henry VIII's so-called 'Rough Wooing' of Scotland laid waste the Border counties. The English commanders, the Earl of Hereford and Sir Ralph Eure ordered around 10,000 cattle and 12,000 sheep to be driven into England as spoils of war. This, however, represented only a fraction of Scotland's livestock. More peaceful conditions were finally ushered in with the 1603 Union of the Scottish and English Crowns. Notwithstanding, trouble continued in the Highlands: also in 1603, the MacGregors 'lifted' 600 beasts from the lands of Colquhoun of Luss on Loch Lomond and fought a bloody battle at Glen Fruin to make good their escape. Most of the clan were proclaimed as outlaws by King James VI & I. Lawlessness in certain parts such as Lochaber would take another hundred years to quell. Even so, at the height of each Jacobite Rising, droves were still threading their way through the hills to markets in the south.

'Nowte' is the old Lallans word for cattle, and with the words 'better to sell nowte than nations' the Earl of Seafield's brother, Patrick Ogilvie, summed up his contempt for the Scots nobles who voted through the 1707 Treaty of Union between the Scottish and English parliaments. The Earl, as the Chancellor of Scotland, presided over that fateful decision. In the aftermath an English army sat menacingly near the border and people rioted, some burning copies of the treaty that had been sent to all corners of the land to be read out at every Mercat Cross.

Trade in cattle was never far from the minds of Scottish lairds. In 1706 the Parliament gathered in Edinburgh for its last session. The majority feared any interruption to the increasingly profitable cross-border cattle trade; many had a huge stake in its success. They held out for an amendment to Article VI of the treaty accepted by the English Parliament. To ensure a free trade in cattle without disadvantage to Scots producers, it included the key phrase:

> From and after the Union no Scots Cattle carried into England shall be liable to any other Duties either on the public or private Accounts than these Duties to which the Cattle of England are or shall be liable within the said Kingdom.[1]

In the mid-seventeenth century droves of two or three hundred were not uncommon and the cattle trade did flourish, compared to many other Scots goods, in the early years of the Union. By the second quarter of the nineteenth century, droves numbered thousands of sheep and cattle and could stretch as far as seven miles on the road to Falkirk Tryst.[2]

Stock came from all over the Highlands and Islands. Records for 1810 show cattle from Islay numbered 2,600, Jura 1,200 and Mull and adjacent islands 2,000.[3] In the early nineteenth century, drovers annually swam 6,000 cattle across the narrows from Kyle Rhea, Skye to the mainland at Glenelg. An estimate of the total cattle stock in the north-west Hebrides would be over 30,000 cattle at that time; about a fifth of the cattle herd in the Hebrides was sold each year. The trade from Lewis via Poolewe used the large open boats that served at other times to transport lime, slate and other cargoes. Onward droving from the north-west Highlands to the Muir of Ord mart would take many of the beasts on the next stage of the long route south, but this heyday was not to last indefinitely.

In 1804, Alexander Campbell gave a warning of changes to come in his polemical poem *The Grampians Desolate:*

> Kintail's famed breed, or that of Skye's green isle
> Spine long and straight, ribs deep, high crested, strong
> Let those true forms be found your herd among;
> So will they thrive when led to Southern keep,
> And prove more gainful far than alien sheep!

He observes that, to the lairds, it would prove more profitable if they could ditch the cattle-rearing population in favour of Linton and Cheviot sheep. From the Borders to the Highlands shepherds were given leases of fertile inland glens where whole townships had been cleared of their inhabitants. In 1792, remembered afterwards as *Bliadhna nan caorach* – 'the year of the sheep', the Strathrusdale folk tried to drive all the sheep out of Ross-shire. Nevertheless, backed by law officers, parish ministers (who were appointed by the lairds) and soldiers based at Fort George, the lairds won.

In 1794 Britain went to war with Revolutionary France. Had the French won, the British landed oligarchy would have, literally, faced the chop and big estates would have been broken up, just as they were in France. Self-interest led the Highland lairds to seek preferment by giving fulsome support to the British imperial wars against the French. They did so by raising several Highland regiments to meet the state's demands for soldiers and sailors.

Additionally, the lairds' parliamentary representatives passed the Passenger Act of 1803 which virtually halted emigration to North America, purportedly on humanitarian grounds, citing poor provision of victuals, water and accommodation on emigrant ships. This had the effect of forcing fares up beyond the level many could afford. Having piloted the measure through Parliament in London, Lord Advocate Hope admitted the following year that it indirectly, yet effectively, dampened 'the rage for emigration to America that had been raised among the people', instancing Lord Selkirk's Canadian settlement schemes.[4]

Post-war economic depression brought about its own ideological volte-face from these same landowners. Instead of defending a high density of tenantry, they began to claim that the Highlands were over-populated. Lucrative sheep ranching tenancies were offered to Lowland shepherds and in particular the tenancies leased by the Countess of Sutherland led to widespread evictions, a pattern repeated throughout the Highlands. In the short space of fifty years sheep succeeded in stripping the remaining fertility of the in-bye lands which had been built up over thousands of years through the better balanced cattle husbandry. To this day, the over-grazing of sheep remains a major cause of the man-made wilderness that characterises so much of the Highlands.

Advocates of estate 'improvement' were either entrepreneurs or exploiters, depending on viewpoint, who practised unfettered free market capitalism. Patrick Sellar, sub-agent to the Sutherland Estates and in-coming sheep tenant of Strathnaver, justifies clearances to Lord Advocate Colquhoun in May 1815:

> Lord and Lady Stafford were pleased humanely, to order a new arrangement in this Country. That the interior should be possessed by Cheviot Shepherds and the people brought down to the coast and placed there in lotts under the size or three arable acres, sufficient for the maintenance of an industrious family, but pinched enough to cause them turn their attention to the fishing. I presume to say that the proprietors ordered this humane arrangement, because, it surely was the most benevolent action, to put these barbarous hordes into a position where they could better Associate together, apply to industry, educate their children, and advance in civilisation.[5]

The following year, a jury of his peers acquitted Sellar. Similar zeal effected enclosure of many glens and also the building of new turnpike roads, blocking the old drove routes. Paradoxically, in 1823 he campaigned vigorously to preserve access to the open drove roads, invoking 'the ancient rights of the people of the Highlands'.

Sheep provided a growing proportion of the droving trade in the first half of the nineteenth century. From around 1770 the Falkirk Tryst, which English dealers found far more convenient, overtook Crieff as the prime market. As the trade increased the Tryst grew to occupy three successively larger sites further out of town. Around 60,000 cattle were sold there in 1794, and, six years later, over 100,000. At the September and October Falkirk marts of 1827, most of the 150,000 cattle sold were driven on to English markets.

In the late eighteenth century, sheep sold in small numbers but during the following decades totals rose rapidly. In 1818, 40,000 were sold at Falkirk; in 1836 the total reached 75,000; and in 1849 close on 200,000 sheep were sold, outnumbering sales of cattle for the first time.

Another blow to cattle trade came about with the creation of deer forests and grouse moors. By 1839 twenty-eight deer forests had been established. By 1900 they numbered 230 in the Highlands alone.[6] Deer-stalking blocked numerous cross-country droving routes and, in the autumn months, shooting clashed with crucial livestock movements.

gives a classic example in his evidence to the 1883 Napier Commission into Crofting in the Highlands and Islands. Describing the droving route from Lochalsh to Muir of Ord mart, some sixty miles in length, he warned that seventeen miles inland from the west coast at Balmacara a shooting tenant had converted the old, easy route by Coireach into a deer sanctuary. This re-routed droves of sheep and cattle over a rough hill pass in order to 'avoid the displeasure of Mr Winnans'. Twenty miles further on through Glen Cannich, which Winnans also rented as a sporting tenant, there were:

> stations fenced with iron wire where droves of cattle or sheep are secured at night to prevent them from trespassing on forest grounds – there being no accommodation provided in the deer forests for the men in charge of these droves nor for any other men. That is tantalising, in as much as there are substantial houses at intervals in this forest. They were built by the hospitable tenantry of former days, but their doors are now closed, apparently in every contempt of shame, humanity and hospitality.

roundly condemned the acquiescence of the landowners Sir

Alexander Matheson and The Chisholm to the wishes of William Winnans, concluding:

> From Balmacara Hotel, Lochalsh to Cannich Bridge Inn, Strathglass, a distance of forty miles, I believe neither drover nor traveller can buy one pennyworth of foods or drink.

Traders from the coast also suffered the exclusion of people from hill paths and the clearance of inland settlements[7]. With the enclosure of every scrap of arable land, drovers faced payment demands for grazing rights at every overnight halt. It is no accident that drove routes were made through high passes and over moorland routes which before the nineteenth century afforded free grazing all along the trails to the cattle trysts.

The great drover John Cameron, known as 'Coirechoille' or 'Corry', rented farms all the way from Lochaber to Falkirk to cut the costs of feed. 'Corry' was born in the parish of Kilmonivaig around 1780, the son of an innkeeper. His first money was made from tending beasts for the passing drovers who drank in his father's inn, and he went on to earn a meagre wage as a barefoot drover's boy before building up a successful droving business. At its peak, he rented around thirty farms in the Lochaber area, having struck a deal with the major local landowner, Cameron of Locheil. Yet despite his business acumen, 'Corry' died in February 1856 with only a small herd of goats to his name and legends abounding as to his droving prowess.

Cattle dealers were hit hard by a 5 to 10 per cent drop in Highland cattle prices reported during the late 1840s when potato blight reached the north-west of Scotland. Due to the appalling Irish famine, English buyers were able to obtain cheaper Irish cattle. However, drovers like Corry mainly sold sheep which maintained buoyant prices even during the Famine years.

The *Transactions of the Highland and Agricultural Society* for 1855 show a total stock of 104,000 cattle grazing in Argyllshire, Inverness-shire, Ross-shire and Sutherland, which between them included all the Hebrides. These were registered as part of the agricultural census that records total cattle numbers for Scotland at 975,000. Both the Highland and Scottish figures had increased marginally to 168,000 and 1,200,000 respectively by 1900. Contrast this with the rapid increase in sheep stock in the Highlands and Scotland as a whole: respectively, 1,900,000 and 5,700,000 in 1855 and 2,000,000 and 7,300,000 by 1900.[8]

The Scottish decline in the cattle trade encouraged the emigration of many families that had been involved in the business from generation to generation. Many left, taking their cattle rearing and droving skills with them.

References

1. Quoted in PH Scott, *Scotland, An Unwon Cause* (Edinburgh, Canongate, 1997), p 215.

2. Alasdair Cameron, 'North Argyll', *Our Greatest Highland Drover, John Cameron, Coirechoille,* reprinted as a pamphlet. Formerly serialised in the Oban Times.

3. Quoted by Una Cochrane, *A Keen Eye, Facts and Folklore of Scottish Highland Cattle* (Highland Cattle Breed Society, 1996).

4. JM Bumstead, *The People's Clearance 1770-1815* (Edinburgh, Edinburgh University Press 1982), pp 129-52.

5. James Hunter, *The Making of the Crofting Community* (Edinburgh, John Donald 1976); and T.M. Devine, *Clanship to Crofters' War* (Manchester, Manchester University Press, 1994), p 27.

6. Willie Orr, *Deer Forests Landlords and Crofters, the Western*

Highlands in Victorian and Edwardian Times (Edinburgh, John Donald, 1982), p 28.

7. R Gibson, *Highland Clearances Trail – a guide* (Evanton, Highland Heritage Educational Trust, 1996), p 34.

8. *Transactions of the Highland and Agricultural Society*, appropriate volumes for years. Full figures as appendix IV in Orr, p 167.

What size were Coirechoille's Highland droves?

Total sales of sheep and cattle at the Falkirk Trysts each year in the 1840s are nearly comparable with the numbers sold at the end of the Texas cattle trails to Kansas in the late 1870s. Evidence from Scottish local newspapers show that sales at the Falkirk Trysts in the 1849 were 130,000 cattle and 200,000 sheep. Of course the full potential of the Western Plains of America allowed more than 350,000 to be driven to Kansas in the best year of the 1880s boom.

Alasdair Cameron FSA Scot. wrote a pamphlet *Our Greatest Highland Drover, John Cameron 'Coirechoille'*, published by the *Oban Times*. He tells us that Corry had attended most of the Highland fairs over the years to buy stock that he drove on to Falkirk each September and October. Corry himself claimed in later life to have done this for fifty consecutive years. Latterly his droves stretched for between five and seven miles along the roads on the way to Falkirk, and were grazed on farms Corry owned or rented.

Stories about Coirechoille are the stuff of legend. He was judged to be the biggest stock-holder in Europe in 1850, apart from Prince Esterhazy of Hungary. Corry protested that the Prince had an unfair advantage, since he had no rent to pay for grazing!

Another story goes that, over a glass of toddy, an admirer once compared Corry to the Duke of Wellington, to which the drover responded, 'The Duke of Wellington was nae doot, a clever man, very clever, I believe. They tell me he was a very good sojer, but then, d'ye see, he had reasonable men to deal with captains and majors and generals that could understand him; plant a company here and a company there at his direction. But I'm not sure after all if he could handle twenty thousand sheep and several thousand black cattle as well that couldna understand one word he said, Gaelic or English, and bring every hoof of them to Falkirk Tryst! I doot it, I doot it very much. But I have often done that.'

CHAPTER 6

Drovers and Dealers

THE SLOW PACE OF the drovers' herds and flocks dictated the distances covered – usually between ten to fifteen miles a day. In Scotland, as in much of Europe, this was carried out by barefoot lads teamed with older drovers who fanned out round the herd. With hazel sticks in hand and dogs at heel they took it easy in the early stages as they found a lead-beast to set the pace for the followers. The drovers were led by a topsman on a sturdy Highland garron who scouted the way ahead, testing swollen rivers, fords, ever on the watch for reivers. He arranged the overnight halts at places where good grazing was available, or in areas with enclosed farms where he paid for grazing in convenient fields. Drovers avoided bridge and road tolls wherever possible so drove routes often took high passes far from habitation. Such was the Minigaig Pass that reached 2,900 feet from Glen Tromie on Speyside to Glen Bruar in Atholl, avoiding tolls in Drumochter Pass. Every extra expense meant the difference between profit and loss. On the drove they ate similar victuals to those used by past Highland armies: a bag of oatmeal soaked in burn water, occasionally bannocks and boiled onions followed by a dram from the ram's horn that each man carried to fortify himself for the rigours ahead.

Agents for the major droving bosses used to walk to the most remote glens and islands to strike bargains directly with the clansfolk. Though they worked a cut-throat trade, their arrival each year was eagerly awaited. Their distinctive dress and demeanour is well captured in *Oran nan Drobhairean* –

'The Drovers Song', said to be composed in the late eighteenth century by Red-haired Murdoch of the Cows, a MacKenzie from Loch Broom in Ross-shire. In 1943 several informants in Sutherland recorded the song, which had been passed down through generations of small farmers and crofters. The recordings are preserved in the School of Scottish Studies at the University of Edinburgh. Red-haired Murdoch described the drovers' dress:

> you wore not the Lowland dress
> that curbs the vigour of the leg with its fastenings
> but the kilt and short hose and the splendid, ample plaid
> that was ever your emblem;
> nor would you exchange it for any other habit...
> He caught the excitement of the local population at the
> arrival of the drovers:
> The sun setting in a golden haze
> and music in the farrow cows' fold.
> Both young and old were amply entertained;
> how cheerfully they danced!
> fish and flesh made the tables creak;
> there was barley bree and brandy...
> we liked the generous man,
> with his kilt and short hose...
> he made it an expensive Whitsuntide for them.[1]

City dwellers were familiar with the sight of Highland drovers arriving at market. But to the eyes of Daniel Defoe, acting as an English Government spy in Scotland around the time of the Treaty of Union in 1707, Highlanders were incongruous figures in the civilised surroundings of the Scottish capital:

> They are all gentlemen, will take affront from no man and insolent

to the last degree. But certainly the absurdity is ridiculous, to see a man in his mountain habit, armed with a broadsword, targe, pistols at his girdle, a dagger and staff, walking down the High Street as upright and haughty as if he were a lord, and withal driving a cow.

John MacInnes, writing in the journal *Scottish Studies* in 1965, noted that drovers retained the right to carry weapons (sword, dirk and musket) and to wear Highland dress under the Disarming Act that banned the tartan with the result that it 'was never worn universally in the Highlands again'. But increasingly drovers took to the road in the 'coarse plaid of a plain brown and white chequer' that became their common garb in the nineteenth century.

MacInnes also remembers how they conducted direct bargaining in glens or trysts, when Gaelic-speaking drovers shook hands, saying, *Siud eadar-iomlaid*, literally, 'it's a mutual exchange'.[2] This conjures up one of the sounds of old-time cattle trysts; and we have several eye-witness accounts of their remarkable colour and size. Unlike the modern mart with its sale ring and weigh-bridge, a vast open space was required to control, bed and process 20,000 cattle such as the young Rob Roy would have witnessed at the Earl of Perth's Crieff Tryst in the 1690s.

The sales methods at Crieff, Falkirk and other trysts were standard. According to a retired drover Dugald MacDougall, they kept the cattle:

in a close bunch, and got them to move round like that. And the buyer was standing outside, and he was seeing them all as they were coming round. And if possible, if there was one that wasn't so good, it was try to keep that one in the middle, let the rest keep him out of sight.

However, he also recalled that each drover had regular buyers.

Once the quality of each drove from a particular locality was assessed, a finisher in the south would know he could rely on the drover's stock from year to year.[3]

At the time of the Falkirk Tryst of October 1849 there were 100,000 sheep for sale in the 200-acre 'well-fenced' field at Stenhousemuir, by Falkirk. One of the best contemporary descriptions of such a tryst is given in Gisbourne's 1854 Essays on Agriculture, which urges readers to:

> ... accompany us to Falkirk Moor on the 2nd Monday or Tuesday in either September or October... and witness a scene to which certainly Great Britain perhaps even the whole world does not afford a parallel... it is not much understated to say around 100,000 sheep collected... Mr Paterson, Mr Sellar, Mr Kennedy and Mr John Cameron of Coirecoille each have several thousands – we have heard this last patriach has 50,000 head of cattle and sheep on his several farms.

> Even those accustomed to the bustle and haggling of the English fair would not suspect the magnitude of the transactions. On the moor adjoining the sheep ground a wooden pent house 5 foot square with the exterior placard announces The Royal Bank of Scotland, others like the British Linen Bank & the Commercial Bank sprang up alongside where letters of credit are exchanged for large notes. A fenced field for the cattle lies next to Larbert at 200 acres in size. Scots drovers on small spirited shaggy ponies used to cattle and sheep mingle with English dealers on large stout horses which tread with more caution. All were ready to bargain.

> Many other tents serve broth, beer and drams where deal making is clinched. The whole field is surrounded by this tented camp with its huge multitude of cattle dealers, drovers, auctioneers, peddlers, jugglers, gamblers, itinerant fruit sellers, ballad singers, and beggars. The uncouth Cumberland jargon and prevailing Gaelic plus the innumerable provincial dialects mingle in one astonishing roar![4]

Gisbourne's evocation smacks of the trail towns at the Kansas railheads in the 1870s, where the 'Johnny Reb' cowboys met Yankee stock buyers, storekeepers and peace officers. A glimpse of the tension between Scots and English drovers was given in a 1936 BBC broadcast entitled *Amongst the Old Men*. Duncan Johnson who had known Iain Black, an old Islayman young at the time of the Battle of Waterloo, recalled:

> Iain was a young, vigorous stripling taking cattle to Falkirk, and he remembered when he was a wee lad, some of the men, then in their old age, who had been at the Battle of Culloden. Many's the tale Iain had about the olden days. He took part in the fights that occurred between Highland drovers and the English drovers at the Falkirk Tryst. He told of how they would harden particular sticks so as to have trusty, vicious weapons ready for any tumult that would break out at that famous market.[5]

The droving industry was by any standards a huge contributor to the Scottish economy that placed many Highland entrepreneurs to the fore. As Coirechoille said, they lived by their wits. Drovers required the skills of a general in battle to take their financial chances on the drove roads to the Falkirk Tryst in its heyday from 1760 to 1860.

Such was the appearance and skills of the drovers sketched by Robert Bontine Cunninghame Graham in the short story 'Falkirk Tryst' in his collection entitled *A Hatchment* (1913). He recalled seeing drovers in his youth in the 1860s camped near his home at Gartmore, Stirlingshire:

> dressed usually in homespun tweeds which smelt of heather and peat smoke and which was so thick that those who wore them look like bears as they lounge heavily along.

> Although inns were built in the nineteenth century to serve the drovers' needs, many still slept out by their herds, wrapped in their plaids on which the frost showed white or dew shone just as it does on a spider's web, their sticks near their hands, they slumbered peacefully.

Argyllshire drovers were still selling there in 1900 when the great Falkirk Tryst reached its last days.[5] By the 1860s, when the railway network was penetrating the Highlands, considerable distances were still covered by drovers as they herded cattle through the hill passes to marts at the railheads. The Highland Railway reached the west coast at Strome Ferry, the port for Skye, in 1870 and Thurso in the far north in 1874. The Caledonian Railway reached Oban in 1880 while the North British Railway reached Fort William in 1894 with its West Highland extension that pioneered reinforced concrete bridges and viaducts to Mallaig in 1901.

The market for the northern Highlands, Am Blar Dubh, Muir of Ord was similarly affected. It flourished for a century. From 1820 onwards cattle from the north-west were gathered there for onward droving to Falkirk. While rail transport replaced longer droves, Muir of Ord still received cattle driven from remote glens. The rail links themselves were to be replaced by lorries or 'cattle floats'. Auction markets with pens and cattle sidings like the one set up at Dingwall superseded Muir of Ord in the 1920s, professional auctioneers replacing man-to-man bargaining. These changes took away much of the colour of the old-time cattle sales.

Colin MacDonald described the drovers' appearance around 1900:

> No two men were dressed alike; each man seemed to have a dis-

tinctive garb of his own... all over there was a picturesque display of colour and individuality in dress and character that is woefully lacking at the ringside in the modern auction mart.[6]

The Muir of Ord market was a two-day event. Sheep were sold on Wednesdays and horses and cattle on Thursdays. School children had a holiday for the sale and were hired by farmers to help with herding. Dealers used the straight, flat, main road through the mart area to show off the paces of their stock. By 1900 the railways had already eliminated the need for huge sales at Muir of Ord Tryst; nevertheless Colin MacDonald was much impressed by the skills he saw there:

farmers and flockmasters, crofters and shepherds, bringing with them thousands of sheep and hundreds of cattle for the purpose of selling to each one and to the farmers and dealers and drovers that came from the south... and what a confusion of sheep and cattle and dogs and shepherds and shouting! To the uninitiated it seemed that never could order come out of that chaos. But order did come eventually; each lot was stanced and the battle of buying and selling began. It was a hard school and it was intensely interesting to watch and listen to the experts at work. With what withering scorn Alastair Breac could point out the defects in a lot of beasts he wanted to buy! And then the convincing manner in which he revealed to prospective purchasers the admirable qualities of that same lot later in the day when he wanted to sell them! A day at the Muir was a liberal lesson in tact, diplomacy, guile, and a hundred other arts useful to existence in this hard world![7]

The Tryst ground at Muir of Ord is now a golf course. There are few reminders of its former use. On the right hand side of what was the main road north is a street of houses where once stood the Caledonian Bank, the Commercial Bank, and an eating house. On the site of the existing golf club was a public house and several wooden buildings. These have now disappeared, along with the sights and sounds of an age-old trade.

References:
1. Sue Jane Taylor, John MacInnes & Graham Watson, *Bho Dhrobhadh Gaidhealach gu Fasaichean Australia – From Highland drove to the Australian Outback* (Dornoch, Dornoch Studio, 1998).
2. J MacInnes, *Scottish Studies* 9, p 204.
3. Quoted by Cregeen, p 155.
3. Thomas Gisbourne, *Essays on Agriculture 1854*, p 15 et seq. quoted in Haldane p 240 as Appendix F – Falkirk Tryst in 1849.
4. Quoted in Cothrom, *Journal of the Adult Gaelic Learners Association CLI*, No. 21, autumn 1999, p 30 'Iomain is Iorghaill' / 'Trysts and Tumults'.
5. Cregeen, p 153.
6. Colin MacDonald, *Echoes of the Glen* (republished along with *Highland Journey as Life in the Highlands and Islands of Scotland* by Aberdeen University Press, 1991). pp 136-37.
7. Ibid, p 137.

Did the Hereford breed come from Strathglass?

Local folklore has it that during the road building and Highland pacification of the mid-eighteenth century; in Strathglass two Hanoverian officers spied a small herd of cattle with white blazes on their faces. These distinctive cattle, called *blaraig* in Gaelic, were of fine proportions and the officers immediately earmarked them for themselves. This appears to have been the practice by officers charged with systematically seizing the goods and belongings of out-lawed Jacobites. Legend has it that they had the cattle driven south to their home in Herefordshire, and they were then crossed with a Devon bull. The progeny are said to have been part of the trials to establish the Hereford cattle breed. Perhaps the Herefords that proved such a successful cross with the Longhorns on the Great Plains of the USA were in part Highland.

CHAPTER 7

The Cattle Trade Goes International

YOU MIGHT BE TEMPTED to believe that life in a remote Highland glen was isolated from outside pressures and influences. Yet for many Gaels a mobile existence was not uncommon. From the earliest times, travellers had brought back new ideas. Soldiers, traders, scholars and drovers all brought home news of politics, fashions and of stock prices. Many settlements lay on the huge network of local and national drove routes, the main lines of communications before metalled roads and railways were built.

The Union of the Scots and English crowns ended Border warfare and opened up trade. Soon raids by Royal Navy press gangs ranged round Britain's coasts, taking many unwilling Highlanders to sail the oceans in the King's service. Some unfortunates were sold either as white slaves or shipped off as criminals to work Caribbean plantations owned by the gentry of both Scotland and England.

Emigrants to the colonies in Ulster, Nova Scotia, Virginia and Carolina further added to the Highlanders' sum of knowledge of the outside world, eventually dispersing the clans themselves, as people saw prospects for a better life in the New World. Extended lines of family communication built a new worldwide network of Gaels.

A series of outside pressures made the seventeenth century one of great instability in the Highlands. Consequent on the successful outreach of royal power, the military class, often the major tenants or tacksmen, began to see the writing on the wall for their role in clan society. Clan chiefs were drawn into mainstream national life. Their legal titles to land were made under the Scots feudal system and registered in Edinburgh. Their sons were educated in English and adopted new Episcopal or Presbyterian forms of worship, or in some cases quietly retained allegiance to the old Catholicism. Loyally, their clansfolk followed suit. Such allegiances lured Highlanders into playing a major part in the civil wars between the Stuarts (who believed in the divine right of kings) and supporters of the Parliament, the Presbyterians of Scotland and puritans of England. This ideological divide between a hierarchical clan structure and the growing influence of parliament drew some Gaels to the Jacobites, supporters of King James VII of Scotland and II of England, forced into exile in 1689 for tampering with the settlement of the Protestant State.

Led by chiefs who backed the very Stuart dynasty that had for centuries attacked Gaelic civilisation as outlandish and rebellious, the Jacobite Highlanders hoped to stave off a worse evil, a Protestant, Hanoverian king. Nevertheless the Hanoverians already had their own Highland adherents, notably among the powerful Campbell clan in the west and the Munros, Sutherlands and MacKays in the far north. The Royalist and Jacobite struggle for ascendancy over Whig parliamentarians spanned the seventeenth century and beyond. After the Treaty of Union in 1707, the Hanoverian dynasty was blamed, or praised, depending on viewpoint, for the carnage of the battle of Culloden in 1746 and the ethnic cleansing of its aftermath.

Large numbers of absentee chiefs living mainly in Edinburgh, stepped up their conspicuous consumption to hob-nob in London court society. By claiming legal title to their land, they shed their age-old clanship responsibilities and began to rack rent their clansmen. Their personal debt spiral often affected which side they took in the Jacobite rebellions. This transformation from clanship to commerce had a troubled passage. Nevertheless cattle-producing areas such as Galloway benefited from the 1707 Treaty of Union by serving the needs of the growing towns of the Lowlands and England. So the need to add Highland beef sources grew with each year.

Cattle for the markets of England had been sourced from all over the British Isles. In the longer run the 'carnivores of London' who, by the Middle Ages were the primary consumers of Welsh cattle, would eventually also require the bulk of Scots and Irish cattle to meet their needs. By 1470 the Welsh droving trade had been organised to supply the needs of London, where the population had already reached 50,000. Before half a millennium of trade was destroyed by the coming of the railways in the 1850s, droving was central to the Welsh economic, cultural and social life. In 1770 cattle were still more important than sheep in Wales and in that year 30,000 cattle were driven through Herefordshire, the first English county crossed en route from North Wales to the English markets. A reputed £16,000 turnover was generated by one partnership of drovers from the Lleyn peninsula; and in the eighteenth century a Welsh drover could earn fifteen times the wage of a labourer.[1]

Such was the growth in demand that stock from each Celtic country was required. Irish beef was shipped and driven to London for centuries, though one of the boosts for Scottish beef trade came with the debarring of Irish cattle from the English market. For over a century after 1667 the 'act against importing cattle from Ireland and other parts beyond the seas' was deeply discriminatory.[2] High tariffs also curtailed the Irish trade with France, Spain and Portugal. War between Great Britain and

France from 1784 to 1815 ended the Continental market through prolonged blockade of French ports by the Royal Navy. Notwithstanding wars, it was bad winters and wet springs which had the greatest effect on the availability of cattle for export. Ill-applied laws were often broken to meet the demands of a rising market in England's towns.

Fluctuations in trade were exemplified by the buyers' market of the Famine Years, 1846-51, when cheap Irish cattle flooded English markets undercutting West Highland cattle prices. In the mid-1850s both countries' beef exports recovered as the urban population of England, Lowland Scotland and the Welsh Valleys grew faster than the century before.

At various times, cattle disease, either in the producer or receiving areas, affected prices. In the 1770s an outbreak in England of cattle plague or rinderpest spread to Scotland, Wales and Ireland. Primitive preventive measures, such as restricting cattle movements, were ineffective. When rinderpest recurred Europe-wide in the 1860s it brought a vigorous response in an age of growing awareness of public health issues. Aberdeen Angus cattle breeder William McCombie led the Scottish fight to halt its spread. His efforts limited the outbreak to some extent but the causes and means of transmission were still not understood in medical terms. There were beef riots in Liverpool when the first imported live US beef arrived in 1867 – the only cheap beef to reach urban populations for many years. American cattle imports were initially small, but by 1870 20,000 tons of live US cattle had arrived in Europe. This new beef source was to alter irrevocably the home-grown beef trade.

Following the end of the Napoleonic Wars in 1815 the slump in demand had ruined many. Thirty years later, Her Majesty's Government produced a controversial Free Trade policy. Sir Robert Peel thereby opened the door to the produce of the colonies and pushed through the repeal of the Corn Laws of 1846. A rising challenge to home production in sheep, cattle, dairy produce and grain was clinched by the fall in transport costs in the 1870s when steam ships replaced sail as the main means of propulsion on the world's oceans, opening up speedy, reliable intercontinental trade.

Live cattle imports from the USA are estimated to have trebled in the three years from 1877 to 1879. Experiments began in 1851 to carry refrigerated goods by rail across the USA. Fresh beef from the pampas was carried in the first dedicated refrigeration ship, the *Frigorifique*, that sailed from Argentina to Le Havre, France in 1878.[3] Two years later the refrigerated vessel the *SS Strathleven* carried the first Texan carcasses from the USA to England.[4]

In 1879 about 60 per cent of total US cattle exports were sent to Britain, adding unexpected fuel to the agrarian bonfire kindled by hard-hit farmers in Ireland, where around 80 per cent of agriculture was concerned with the cattle trade. This crisis fuelled demands for Irish Home Rule. In its wake, Scotland and Wales also began to develop Home Rule aspirations, connected to concerns about securing autonomous agricultural production. A January 1877 editorial in a Dublin newspaper, the *Freeman's Journal*, commented, 'The economic condition of Ireland at this moment is a precarious one, and this day twelve months it is at least possible that it may be a desperate one'. It noted with foreboding, 'a means has been discovered of importing American beef in good condition and at a cheap rate'.

Droves the length of Britain had developed an international trade across the centuries. This was rudely eclipsed by refrigerated steamships bringing 169,000 tons of cheaper US beef into the

British Isles in 1880, on a more humane basis than the continuing live meat trade across the Atlantic. With Australia, New Zealand and Argentina adding their produce to European butchers' slabs, a global trade in essential foodstuffs was made manifest.

References
1. John Davies, *A History of Wales* (London, Penguin, 1990), pp 213, 260, 317, 410.
2. LM Cullen, *Economic History of Ireland Since 1660* (London, Batsford, 1987), p 27.
3. CIA Ritchie, *Food in Civilisation: How History Has Been Affected by Human Tastes* (New York, Beaufort Books, 1981), p 187.
4. J Turrentine Jackson, *The Enterprising Scot – Investors in the American West after 1873* (Edinburgh, EUP, 1968), p 74.

CHAPTER 8

Cattle Displace Buffalo and the Plains Indians

THE FIRST BUFFALO REACHED America by the land bridge route from Asia over 200,000 years ago. Archaeological evidence from the Illinoisian glacial age reveals them to be stout, long-horned animals. By the early eighteenth century around seventy-five million of their smaller descendants teemed on the Western Plains of North America. At its greatest, their range had included the wooded foothills of the Appalachian Mountains further east.[1]

Livestock rearing was practised by the Vikings, who colonised Greenland, despite its demanding climate, for five hundred years. But their colony only survived during the relatively warmer era that ended around 1500 AD. Around 1010 AD one Greenland-based leader, Kalsefni, took livestock of all kinds to Vinland, the area which includes Nova Scotia and New England, with the aim of making a permanent settlement on the American mainland. While we are unsure that any animals survived the short Viking stay, there are stories of cattle surviving shipwrecks of settlers on the American coasts in subsequent centuries.

The main introduction of cattle and horses to the American continent occurred with the arrival of Christopher Columbus at Hispaniola in 1494. Gregorio de Villalobos shipped the first herd of Spanish cattle from the West Indies to the Mexican mainland in 1521.[2] Six heifers and a young bull of sturdy Andalusian stock, described as 'sharp horned fighters, fast as wild deer', arrived in Vera Cruz with the Spanish Conquistadors. Over the next three centuries they were herded in extensive ranches by *vaqueros*, the Spanish-trained mestizo cowboys. In the 1560s, cattle ranching slowly spread through Mexico and Florida into what became Texas.[3] By the early 1700s, 100,000 cattle were tended by the Spanish missions or had escaped into the Texas bush, where huge wild herds roamed the Great Plains, land once exclusive to the buffalo. Further west, in 1834, figures show 31,000 mission *vaqueros* tending 400,000 cattle in Spanish California.[4]

Anglo-Saxon migrants from the United States, moving into Texas in order to extend the grazing for their cattle herds, began to shoot the buffalo. The Mexican authorities had no strategic development plans for Texas and encouraged settlement by Americans from the beginning of the nineteenth century, stipulating that land ownership was conditional on their being, or becoming, Catholic. One of the earliest cattle brands to be registered at Gonzales, Texas was by Richard H Chisholm in 1832. In 1836 the infant Republic of Texas declared its independence from Mexico; much of its wealth was based on its 6:1 cattle to human ratio. Anglos and Mexicans increasingly contested the available grazing lands as American business acumen tried to harvest the wild Texas cattle that were declared the property of whoever could brand them.

Over the next thirty years the location of new markets for Texas cattle went through several phases. In the 1840s the Gulf of Mexico ports at Shreveport and New Orleans were targeted. In 1846 a herd was driven to Ohio and in 1848 the California Gold Rush was served with Texas cattle driven 1,500 miles to the west. During the 1850s, cattle were driven as far as New York, but gradually, eastern States set up a quarantine line to protect domestic farm stock from the endemic cattle fever carried by Texas cattle from the Gulf coast. At the same time, demand for buffalo hides and tongues led buffalo skinners to leave carcasses strewn across the plains for the vultures and coyotes. Eventually they gathered the carcasses for tallow, hooves and horns required in the industrialising north-east USA. This wasteful practice only eased with the arrival of railroad construction gangs out West in the later 1860s. Buffalo meat from each carcass was fully exploited. In the face of wholesale slaughter, the once-great buffalo herds were divided into rapidly diminishing north and south fractions whose destruction provided sport for the rich easterners and European royalty seeking adventure on the Great Plains.

The aftermath of the American Civil War in 1865 brought about the complete displacement of buffalo by range cattle. Peace provided opportunities to sell livestock to the war-ravaged but victorious and hungry north. Huge wild herds of unbranded cattle had been left much to themselves during the hostilities on the Texas Plains. A similar herd in the 1840s had belonged to Samuel A Maverick, who inadvertently lent his name to the language when he accepted a debt paid in cattle and then left his payment to multiply in the swampy coastal plains of Matagorda County, Texas. Soon all unbranded cattle in the area were referred to as 'Maverick's'. By 1865 the term, like the cattle themselves, had spread far and wide.

When the railroads extended west in the race to span the continent, their arrival in Kansas, en route for California and Oregon, was to open up the previously little-regarded Western Frontier. Several businesspeople saw the potential out on the Plains. At Christmas 1865 the plentiful Texas Longhorns, worth a mere $5 in Texas, could fetch $40 if driven to the Chicago markets. The first successful cattle trail to a railhead was based on the wagon road marked out by Tennessee-born half-Cherokee Jesse Chisholm who traded from Kansas with Indian Territory – now part of the State of Oklahoma. It was Illinois-born Joseph McCoy who, in 1867, saw the potential of setting up cattle pens and a Drovers Cottage Hotel at Abilene, Kansas. This site had, until then been simply a collection of huts on the route of the Kansas Pacific Railroad. McCoy's success in enticing cattlemen from Texas to drive their herds over the extended Chisholm Trail set a pattern for twenty legendary years of the western cattle drives. Thereafter, cross-bred cattle of much improved quality were demanded by the market, replaced the Longhorn on consumers' plates.[5]

The routes taken by Scots and other settlers to reach the Wild West were many and various. Jesse Chisholm is a case in point. Jesse's grandfather John D Chisholm arrived in South Carolina in 1777 to join the trading business of his father, who had arrived some years previously. John was accused of some questionable land deals in Florida and Georgia but eventually traded with the Cherokee Indians in North Carolina and Tennessee. In 1814 he represented the tribe to the government in Washington DC. His son Ignatius, also a slave trader, was married to the daughter of Cherokee Chief Cork Tassle.[6] Their son Jesse became a trader and Indian representative. He moved west with the clearance of the tribes from their homelands in the fertile east to the arid plains beyond the Mississippi River where he marked out his wagon road from Kansas to Indian Territory. Unfortunately he died of cholera in 1868 without knowing his name had been given to a major cattle trail based on his marked-out route, which was later extended further into Kansas to open up the huge market for Texas cattle.

By the 1880s many sons of better-off Scots would become Western cattlemen, forming or managing giant new ranch companies. Others, in search of a steady wage, sought work on cattle and sheep ranches, some on the regular pay-roll and others as migrant workers. Old skills had already been transferred from Europe to America; indeed the vast clearout of Highland small farmers from Scotland was a major source. Witness the development of arable and stock farming adapted for the hotter conditions of the eastern USA. New settlers on the Great Plains would have had many old stock rearing and marketing skills to draw on from a century or more of American experience. However, cattle ranching was largely learned from, but never credited to, the Mexican *vaqueros*.

In the ruins of the Confederacy the more adventurous cattlemen and farmers saw the potential of Texas and the West as a large-scale version of their inherited experience, free from old constraints whether in feudal Europe, or in the now over-crowded, original US colonies. Chisholms, Chisums, Campbells, MacDonalds, MacKenzies, Clays, Grants, MacLeays, Anguses, Irvines and many other Scots came to the fore in establishing the cattle empires that were built on the Great Plains following the near-extinction of the buffalo.

The decline from around seventy-five million animals in 1700 to a few thousand in 1880 was an awesome tragedy for the species. Credited with saving the last of the pure-bred buffalo was one successful Scots rancher, James 'Scotty' Philip.[7] But it is hard to contemplate the scale of destruction of the buffalo herds by the settlers, railroads and cattlemen on the American Frontier.

Scots followed many trades out West. A large number of Highlanders were among the first fur traders. Others were buffalo hunters, cattlemen and shepherds. Many had close relations with the indigenous nomadic tribes. In the 1840s a Scots fur trader, Angus MacDonald, married into the Nez Percé tribe. Angus and his family set up home raising cattle near Missoula on the Flathead Indian Reservation in western Montana after he left the Hudson Bay Company. His son Duncan and another half Scot, half Indian, Billy Irvine, along with eleven cowboys, a chuck wagon and a herd of wild Longhorns, trailed a thousand miles south to Cheyenne, Wyoming in the fateful summer of 1876 when the US Cavalry were trying to avenge the Custer massacre.[8] They dared not drive a direct route to the railhead through east Montana for fear of losing their herd in the Lakota and Cheyenne Indian War along the Little Bighorn, where, in June that year, Colonel George Armstrong Custer and two hundred of the Seventh Cavalry had 'died a-running' from three thousand Sioux and Cheyenne warriors. A Hudson Bay employee, Angus met his wife Catherine whilst setting up fur trading activities in western Montana in the 1840s. He is said to have been a direct descendent of the MacDonalds of Glencoe, a 'tribe' which suffered 'murder under trust', the slaughter of forty men, women and children by orders of King William of Orange's British Government in 1692.

Both the Hudson Bay Company and North West Company instructed their employees to make friendly relations with native Americans so as to encourage the fur trade. However, a sizeable number of Scots who took Indian wives incurred the company's displeasure because they praised native culture and refused to dump their new families and move on when ordered to. Some eventually took their wives back to the islands of Orkney and Lewis in Scotland. McDonald Peak and McDonald Lake in Mission Valley, Montana are testament to Angus

MacDonald's lasting influence in his new home area. Popular myths of the Wild West play down the more intimate contact of American tribes and white settlers. Trade and intermarriage often took place during times when native Americans and the US Government came to blows.

Scotty Philip, who was born at Auchness Farm, Dallas in Morayshire in 1858, joined an elite colony in Kansas as a labourer when he was sixteen. On the death of its founder, George Grant, he went prospecting for gold and silver in the Black Hills of Dakota. Marriage to a native American made him brother-in-law to Crazy Horse, the famed warrior leader of the Lakota tribe. Scotty was only one of several Scots who married native Americans and also had sympathy for their plight. Marriage assured him access to the Indian lands guaranteed by treaty but rumoured to be rich in gold. Like many, he failed to find pay dirt, but with his growing family he made a big success of ranching near Pierre, South Dakota, where he built up a herd of pure-bred buffalo after purchasing fifty from the estate of Pete Duprée in 1900. Soon these bred and were able to restock Yellowstone National Park, zoos and many other ranches. Tom Bryan notes in *Rich Man, Beggar Man, Indian Chief*:

> Scotty Phillip rounded up the remaining buffalo and kept them in an enclosure on his ranch in South Dakota. He retained only pure-bred animals and soon established a breeding herd. In 1906 the US Government gave him 3,500 acres for pasturing buffalo. This park soon became a major tourist attraction and Phillip sold breeding pairs as well as developing buffaloes for meat. Although other herds survived, most of the pure bloodline for this nearly extinct animal came from Jamie Phillip's original herd.[8]

At the time of his death in 1911, aged 53, Scotty Phillip was rightly dubbed 'The Buffalo King'; his herd of pure-bred buffalo numbered 400 and as the basis of most modern herds that recovered to number around 95,000 in 1990.

Not only the white settlers but also Plains Indians chiefs were interested in cattle-rearing in the wake of the buffalo's destruction. Mato Gleska, or Spotted Bear, made some far-sighted remarks on the eve of the Custer campaign:

> Our Great Father has a big safe, and so have we. The hill is our safe. We want seventy million dollars for the Black Hills. Put the money away some place at interest so we can buy livestock. That is the way white people do.

Cattlemen like Charles Goodnight cross-bred cattle and buffalo. An Illinois man, he joined the Texas Rangers when they moved west and became a doyen of cattle ranchers and breeders. He invented the chuck wagon; eventually he crossbred Herefords with Longhorns to develop better beef cattle, and also tried to cross buffalo with Longhorns, the result being infertile cattaloos. In partnership with Irish landowner John Adair he set up the JA Ranch in 1877 at Palo Duro, in the Texas Panhandle; it boasted one million acres and 100,000 head of cattle. However, he did save some buffalo from extinction as a result, and his small herd was later preserved for the nation after his passing in 1929 at the age of ninety-three.

By 1900 the buffalo throughout the West had become virtually extinct. For every buffalo rounded up, millions had been slaughtered to make way for the profitable range cattle, 600,000 of which were driven over the Chisholm Trail from Texas to Abilene in 1871, its most profitable year. In the early 1880s, 350,000 head would reach the Dodge City railhead annually.[9]

By 1880, the US census identified 800,000 range cattle in

Texas and 250,000 in the northerly ranges of Wyoming. The 1883 census shows that there were five million cattle in Texas and one million in Wyoming. The grandson of a Scots Highland emigrant had traded in Indian Territory and opened up the route that saved the Texas economy after the devastation of the Civil War. The Chisholm Trail named after him opened up markets in the north-eastern USA and Europe, and allowed passage of stock to open the northern ranges of Wyoming and Montana, building an even bigger American cattle industry.

The *Edinburgh Courant* estimated that US ranges would soon produce as many cattle as Great Britain, France, Germany and Russia put together. Naturally, the US Department of Agriculture viewed this prospect with great satisfaction. The stage was set for major foreign investment, half of which was to be organised and funded from Scotland.

References

1. David A Dary, *The Buffalo Book: The full saga of the American animal* (Ohio, Swallow Press & Ohio University Press, 1974 and 1989), p 5.

2. Jon E Lewis, *The Mammoth Book of the West* (London, Robinson, 1996), p 147.

3. Dee Brown, *The American West* (New York, 1994), p 42.

4. RW Slatta, *Cowboys of the Americas* (New Haven, Yale University Press, 1990), p 22.

5. Don Cusic, *Cowboys and the Wild West: An A-Z Guide from the Chisholm Trail to the Silver Screen* (New York, Fact on File, 1994), p 187.

6. Stan Hoig, *Jesse Chisholm: Ambassador of the Plains* (Colorado, University of Colorado, 1991).

7. James Hunter, *Glencoe and the Indians* (Edinburgh, Mainstream Publishing, 1996), pp 30-31.

8. Tom Bryan, *Rich Man, Beggar Man, Indian Chief: Fascinating Scots in Canada and America* (Insch, Thistle Press, 1997), p 55.

9. Wayne Gard, *The Chisholm Trail* (Norman, University of Oklahoma Press, 1954), p 260.

Chisholms in the West

Our interest in the Scottish origins of cattlemen Jesse Chisholm, John Chisum and Richard Chisholm poses the classic question: How can we be sure of Scottish roots when written records are fragmentary before 1800? Crucial information is to be found in parish registers, family papers and local lore.

The Chisholm family was of Norman French origin. They are recorded as land-holders in the Scottish Borders in the fourteenth century. As a reward for military service for the Scots King they were married into the barony of The Aird, which covers the Glen Glass area west of Inverness. This led to Chisholm clan history developing in that predominantly Gaelic society.

At the time of the Ulster Plantation under orders from King James VI and I, many Lowland and Argyllshire Scots of a Protestant persuasion were enlisted. The other branch of Chisholms who had remained in the Scots Borders was amongst those adventurers. They in turn emigrated to North America a century later to find better prospects and, during the American War of Independence, many Ulster Scots in North Carolina supported the Revolutionaries.

Catholic Jacobite Highlanders escaping in the aftermath of 1746 to North America often quite paradoxically took the Loyalists side and became victims of another lost cause. The South Carolina Gaels divided more evenly. Thereafter the routes taken by settlers drawn West of the Appalachians and later beyond the Mississippi are many and various.

Jesse Chisholm's roots wend through the Southern States; his family were slave owners and also married Cherokees, one of the five Civilised Tribes who lived there. Jesse's father was named Ignatius. Tantalisingly, there is a St Ignatius Well in Strath Glass. Significantly, local lore in Strath Glass speaks of three Chisholm brothers who reached Texas. Their name change to the phonetic Chisum is probably linked with the famous cattleman John Chisum who was himself born in Tennessee. It is not known if Jesse Chisholm and John Chisum were related.

'But the queys was goot'. A 19th-century pen-and-ink drawing of typical
Highland kyloes.
(From *Sketches of Highland Character – Sheep Farmers and Drovers*,
Edinburgh, Edmonton and Company, nd.)

Feill a Loch na madaidh. Lochmaddy Tryst, North Uist late 19th-century.
(The Highland Council, Highland Folk Museum Collection)

Sheep driven from mart through Dingwall High Street. This 1950s photo in the Ross-shire market town indicates why sheep and cattle often broke shop windows and carried off clothing on their horns.

(Iain Sutherland, photographer, Dingwall)

Swimming cattle across the Sound of Vatersay to Barra. A photo of crofting activity fifty years ago in the Western Isles (Reg Allan, by kind permission of Frank G. Thompson)

Landing cattle on Barra after swimming the Sound of Vatersay.
(Reg Allan, by kind permission of Frank G. Thompson)

Jessie Chisholm. Chisholm's wagon road from Kansas to Indian Territory formed the basis, in reverse, of the famous Chisholm Trail over which millions of cattle were driven to market. It was named posthumously.
(University of Oklahoma)

John Clay. Clay was a Berwickshire-born Scottish commission agent and ranch manager. Clay made a lifelong career in the Western cattle business including presidency of the Wyoming Stock Growers Association in controversial times in the late 1880s.
(University of Wyoming collection)

Postcard view of Achiltibuie and reverse addressed to K Graham, c/o BHS Company, Crow Agency, Montana, USA). (By kind permission of Tom & Valerie Bryan)

Murdo MacKenzie. Manager of the Matador Land and Cattle Company surveying stock at market (South-West Collection, Texas Technical University, Lubbock).

'They named a town for Murdo'. Water tower, Murdo, South Dakota. Cattle from the Matador ranch were raised in Texas and fattened in northern States, e.g. on rented land in the Pine Ridge Indian Reservation, South Dakota.

(Photo by Tom Bryan, 1998)

Cowboy Outfits. Gibson and Rintoul family group Christmas 1954, Seton Terrace, Dennistoun, Glasgow. Author wearing white hat! Apparently that Christmas in our street there were presents of eight little cowboys outfits and only one Indian girl outfit. Perhaps the Wild West interest was stimulated by the visit of Roy Rogers, his wife Dale Evans and his horse Trigger to play the Empire Theatre.

(Photo by the author's father, the late John Gibson)

Be a true friend; never knock,
always boost.

OLD MONTANA

Take me back to old Montana
Where there's plenty room and air;
Where there's cotton-wood an' pine trees,
Bitter-root an' prickly-pear;
Where there ain't no pomp nor glitter
Where a shillin's called a "bit;"
Where at night the mag-pies twitter,
Where the injun fights were fit.

Take me back where the sage is plenty,
Where there's rattle-snakes and ticks;
Where a stack of "whites" costs twenty,
Where they don't sell gilded bricks;
Where the old Missouri river
An' the muddy Yellowstone
Make green patches in the Bad Lands
Where old Sitton' Bull was known.

Take me where there ain't no subways
Nor no forty-story shacks;
Where they shy at automobiles,
Dudes, plug hats an' three-rail tracks;
Where the old sun-tanned prospector
Dreams of wealth an' pans his dirt;
Where the sleepy night-herd puncher
Sings to steers and plys his quirt.

Take me where there's diamond hitches,
Ropes an' brands an' ca'tridge belts;
Where the boys wear shapps fer britches,
Flannel shirts an' Stetson felts.
Land of alfalfa an' copper!
Land of sapphire an' gold!
Take me back to dear Montana,
Let me die there when I'm old.
　　　　　　　　　—By J. Campbell Cory

This postcard of the quaint poem is addressed to James Stewart, Billings,
Montana. His son Kenneth Stewart of Polglass, Coigach, gave it to Tom Bryan.
James Stewart had intended to settle permanently in Montana but a visit to
Scotland in 1913 was prolonged by the outbreak of World War I and he never
returned to Montana.

Achiltibuie Cowboys. Group photo taken in Billings, Montana c. 1900 where many Highland cowboys went to work on contract. Big Angus, Murdo's neighbour, top right. Murdo MacLean, author of Gaelic song Mo Shoraidh Leis a' Choigich, Leaving Coigach, written in Montana, top left.
(By kind permission of Donald J Campbell, Polglass, Achiltibuie, Ross-shire, Scotland)

Robert Bontine Cunninghame Graham. On horseback in San Antonio,
Texas 1882 with his wife Gabriella, brother Charles, on leave from the
Royal Navy, plus his fox terrier 'Jack'. Taken during Don Roberto's attempts at
ranching in a far from settled State.
(From the private collection of Lady Jean Polwarth – Charles's grand daughter)

CHAPTER 9

Invest Out West!

JAMES BRISBIN WAS THE author of an 1881 best-seller, *The Beef Bonanza, or How to Get Rich on the Plains*. It had phenomenal sales particularly in Britain. Already huge ranch companies built up by successful settlers in Texas and New Mexico were seeking markets by driving cattle to the eastern United States. Texas cattle businesses came into their own through the railroad expansion into Kansas, but farming settlers, who also pushed west, demanded quarantine lines to protect their vulnerable stock from Texas cattle fever carried by the Longhorns. The cattle drives were directed further and further west by the state authorities, to hastily erected new towns at Abilene, Hays, Caldwell, Elsworth and eventually Dodge City. More often than not cattle ranchers made some profits, though markets often fluctuated. In some years, if the eastern market was glutted, they could extend the cattle drives to new ranching country in Colorado, Wyoming and Montana, where investors sought to build even greater empires.

Richard King, born to immigrant Irish parents in New York, was one of the most successful of the earlier Texas ranchers. When he died in 1885, his will showed he owned 1.27 million acres and had 40,000 cattle, 6,600 horses and 1,200 sheep and goats.[1] He turned to ranching after an entrepreneurial career transporting cotton in river boat steamers along the Rio Grande and across the Gulf of Mexico. He was noted for progressive cattle rearing practices such as crossing Longhorns with British breeds, increasing the value of their beef.

A cattleman of Scots descent, Henry H 'Hank' Campbell, born in North Carolina in 1840, moved to Texas before the Civil War where he learned to drive cattle. In 1878 he made a big profit in Chicago where, during a banquet, he was able to convince fellow cattlemen, meat packers, stockyard contractors and railroad executives to invest. He showed that the $9 per head purchase price for Longhorn steers in Texas could be increased to $23 at sales in Chicago. He gathered five partners and $50,000 investment and set up the Matador Ranch, based in the Texas Panhandle at Ballard Springs, south-west of the JA Ranch. He bought his first livestock from John Chisum (originally spelled Chisholm) of Lincoln County, New Mexico. Chisum had founded his cattle empire in 1867 following a career as a contractor and builder. He is most famous for his association as the employer of Billy the Kid in the murderous Lincoln County 'War' of 1878-79.

These huge ranching projects had only become possible through the slaughter of the buffalo herds and the confining of Indian peoples in Government-run reservations. The cattlemen had good reason to be grateful to one US Army officer, Col. Ranald Slidell MacKenzie. MacKenzie was born in New York in 1840, the son of Highland parents. He saw action in the western territories, defeating Quanah Parker and the Comanches in 1874 to free up the Staked Plains of the Texas Panhandle for ranch development.

Speculators wrote up glowing prospectuses contacting potential investors, among them Scots companies which had already profited from the farm mortgages of settlers who pushed west and from railroad stock as the trans-continental network was built up. It was a short step to investing heavily in cattle ranching. BH 'Barbecue' Campbell had been a Shorthorn cattle breeder in Illinois and had gained his name from running the BQ herd in Kansas. In 1879 he was employed to develop a Texas ranch company, set up by the Capital Freehold Land and Investment Co. Ltd., capitalised at £3m. Its board included the Earl of Aberdeen, Henry Seton-Kerr MP and the Marquis of Tweeddale as chairman. 'Barbecue' Campbell became famous for giving a sound business basis to the huge XIT ranch named by the Capital Co. after its investors, 'ten in Texas'.

The 1870 Naturalisation Act had eased British investment abroad. The British Royal Commission of 1879, studying the effects of American imported beef on home producers, concluded that UK bloodstock was not threatened by inferior Texas Longhorns. It also reported that there was a great deal of money to be made for British investors by grazing cattle on the 'self-made hay' of the free public range in the American West.

One Royal Commissioner of note was John Clay, a tenant farmer of the Duke of Roxburgh in Berwickshire and father of one of leading agents for Scots investors in cattle in the US West over the next thirty years. Thanks to his influence, his son, also John, was employed on research for the Commissioners during that time. The report in 1881 indicated that capital investment in the American cattle industry in the previous ten years earned over 33 per cent profit annually. Along with Brisbin's well-timed book, the Royal Commission report stimulated a surge of investment from Edinburgh, Dundee and London in the western US cattle industry. It was a period of high profits from industrial investments in Britain: British business was expansive and confident, despite an agricultural depression in the 1880s caused by British investment capital flowing towards the foreign competitors of British agriculture. Such investment was underpinned by the share profits of export-based industrial and manufacturing businesses, which had been achieved through poor wages and conditions.

In the 1880s it is calculated that $45 million (then equivalent to £9 million) was gathered from Scots shareholders for cattle company investment in the American West, about half of the total foreign investments in the cattle business. John Clay Jnr commented, 'The British companies were mostly floated in Scotland and it is simply marvellous how freely the Scottish investors loaded up with securities of this character'.[2]

The longest-lived Scots-owned American range cattle company was founded in Dundee: the Matador Land and Cattle Company, bought in December 1882 from H H Campbell's Ballard Springs enterprise of the same name. The first chairman, William Robertson, was a successful Tayside engineer. Most of the £2 million invested came from stock bought by investors from around Dundee. The Earl of Airlie had previously advised his countrymen to invest 'big', and the Matador's shareholders heeded this advice. Trading began on the Staked Plains, where the company owned about 100,000 acres, and held grazing 'privileges' on a further 1.5 million acres.

WM Pearce noted in his history of the company that one condition of the sale was that two of the former owners were to be brought onto the board; in due course they received a quarter of the stock in part payment for the ranch properties. This coincided with the directors taking full control from the new headquarters in Dundee rather than from Ballard Springs, Texas.[3]

The Matador's history exemplifies the difference between Scots caution and English speculation. The Hansford, Texas, Westerne and Swan concerns were all part of a rapid Scottish investment boom. Many English-based companies, such as the one pioneered by Moreton Frewen on the Powder River, Wyoming, did not buy the land and had few assets when times got tough, as they did in 1887. But the Matador Co., like most Scots companies, was property-based and therefore commercially more stable.[4] Severe drought in 1883, and during every decade thereafter, made the need for such prudence apparent. These companies, registered and organised from Scotland emerged so strongly in North America because generations of Scots had invested time, money and energy in animal husbandry and the droving trade. They already had invaluable hands-on expertise. The men who guided these ranching companies, such as John Clay from Berwickshire and Murdo MacKenzie, from Ross-shire, were to become amongst the greatest of Western cattlemen.

References

1. Lawrence Woods, *British Gentlemen in the West: The Era of the Intensely English Cowboy* (London, Robson Books, 1990).

2. John Clay, *My Life on the Range* (privately printed 1924, reprinted Norman, University of Oklahoma Press, 1962).

3. WM Pearce, *The Matador Land and Cattle Company* (Norman, University of Oklahoma, 1964), p 11.

4. JT Jackson, p 95.

CHAPTER 10

A Scots Middleman Out West – John Clay

JOHN CLAY SNR HAD radical views on landlords and their stranglehold on Scottish life. Although he was a leading agricultural commentator of his day, even he could not pay the rent increase demanded in 1876 by the Duke of Roxburgh. Like many a Scots tenant before him he lost all his investment on improvements, in the days before the Agricultural Holdings Acts. His son John inherited his father's jaundiced view of lairds and frequently aired them during his long career in America,[1] particularly after his sacking by the Swan Company in 1896.

Like many a Scot, John Jnr emigrated to find his fortune and apply his training as a land surveyor on behalf of UK clients with landed interests in western America. Twenty-three when he first visited Canada in 1874, he became the manager of George Brown's Bow Park Farm and was later commissioned by Scottish investors to investigate properties for potential land and cattle business ventures. He built a career as the expert middleman, trouble-shooter and occasional manager of cattle interests, working mainly for Scots employers. Joining the Wyoming Stock Growers Association (WSGA) in 1882, he surveyed properties and herds in many states and territories throughout the 1880s and 1890s. Chicago was his base. His livestock commission business, initially a partnership with his brother-in-law W H Forrest, reverted to the title John Clay & Co. after Forrest's death.

Investment in the Wild West by Scottish aristocrats and

businessmen brought Clay prosperity, even in hard times. He cut a sharp deal, taking a percentage from the ranch investors' expected commission on the cattle delivered to the Chicago stockyards. He held scathing views of competitors and critics, and in particular of the early aristocratic English speculators – evidently overlooking their willingness to innovate in new technology and to bring pure-bred Aberdeen Angus and Hereford stock from Britain to improve their herds.

Clay's memoir, *My Life on the Range*, published in Chicago in 1924, is full of insights about the ups and downs of the cattle business. He was certainly not shy to express his opinions and he did not hide his prejudices. Nevertheless, this Scots-born 'buggy boss' gave a classic description of the western scene which incidentally testified to his hands-on style of management that eventually enraged his overseas bosses. Of the great cattle drives he wrote:

> You see a steer's head and horns silhouetted against the skyline, and then another and another, till you realise it is a herd. On each flank is a horseman. Along come the leaders with a swinging gait, quickening as they smell the waters of the muddy river.

Perhaps Clay's most controversial exploit was his part in the cattle crisis in Wyoming following the great storm in the winter of 1886-87. Blizzards had destroyed whole cattle herds, forcing liquidations on many cattle firms including Moreton Frewen's Powder River Company. Clay, as president of WSGA, took charge of his fellow members, who had been used to meeting in the cattlemen's palatial HQ, the Cheyenne Club, which succumbed in the crash of 1887. Wishing to maintain the open range system, they opposed settlers who, under the Homestead Acts, had been increasing their claims every year. With public land surveying almost complete, the 1890 census could no longer define a frontier between settled and wild land.

Settlers and small ranchers were tempted to add a few unbranded cattle to increase their herds. By the late 1880s rustlers were using running irons – illegal, short branding irons which could swiftly change a registered brand on range cattle. They were able to re-brand mavericks herded into secluded spots before being found out by cowhands and stock detectives employed by the big companies.

With stock losses mounting, the WSGA wanted all those in possession of short irons to be prosecuted. The Wyoming legislature passed a Mavericks Bill in 1884, yet courts in Buffalo, capital of Johnson County, North Wyoming, were still unable to make charges stick and in some cases the miscreants were freed. Nate Champion, a small rancher and ex-cowhand for a WSGA member, became a prime target of the big ranchers when they resolved to take unilateral action in the autumn of 1891.

John Clay was involved in discussions about proposed vigilante activity with Major Frank Wolcott, a US Marshall and rancher in Wyoming Territory. He had lost most of his stock in the 1887 blizzards and was deeply in debt to Clay, who later described him as an 'honest, clean, rapid Republican with a complete absence of tact'. As a law enforcer, Frank Wolcott faced an array of opponents on the frontier, many of them desperate to get a start in the cattle business. Some were Texas cowboys who had drifted north with droves of cattle to settle in Wyoming Territory; others were Southern Democrats, ex-Confederates, and, in the sociologists jargon, 'social bandits' who perhaps justified their criminal acts with a kind of Robin Hood morality, challenging the established ranchers' belief that they deserved a monopoly of rights on the rapidly closing frontier.

Originally, an enterprising cowhand employee might progress to becoming a cattleman in his own right. But after the 1886–87 drought and blizzards, when cattle grew scarcer and therefore more valuable, mavericking and rustling became much more likely expedients to kick-start a career. Other enforced changes included the more costly Midwest cattle production method, based on the growing of winter fodder, which superseded the haphazard, free-range Texas system. Sheep production also grew and offered poorer settlers a cheaper investment opportunity. As a result, close-cropped sheep grazings began to encroach on the cattle ranges.[2]

Among the settlers of Wyoming was Ella Watson, known as 'Cattle Kate'. Clay accused her of receiving stolen cattle in return for her favours. She and her husband Jim Averill, a storekeeper, were early targets of the WSGA. His 'crime' was to write scathing criticisms of the big ranchers. In the *Casper Weekly Mail*, Averill had denounced Stock Growers member Albert J. Bothwell, whose land adjoined his homestead. He attacked the cattle barons for their greed and monopolistic power. In July 1889, following verbal warnings from Association officers, Watson and Averill were dragged from their cabins by masked men and hanged. Clay distanced himself from these lynchings describing them as a 'horrible piece of business'. However, speaking for many Western cattle barons, he asked, 'what are you to do? Are you to sit still and see your property ruined with no redress in sight?'

The ambush and killing of a WSGA cattle detective, George Henderson, followed in October 1890 and upped the ante. He was shot at Three Crossings on the Sweetheart Creek on the old Oregon Trail. It was rumoured that he had been a ringleader in the Averill/Watson lynching. Clay praised Henderson as a man who 'would rather hunt a thief than eat'. On 1 November WSGA employees, former Johnson County Sheriff Frank Canton, Fred Coates, Joe Elliott and Bill Lykens were involved in a gun battle with Nate Champion and some of his friends. Champion's fears of being a marked man were heightened when Association 'hit man' Frank Canton and another man were alleged to have ambushed and shot 'Ranger' Jones and John Tisdale, two of Champion's small rancher friends, near Buffalo. The settlers of Johnson County feared a major purge and in popular lore Canton was found guilty and only extricated from a trial by high-powered WSGA lawyers. But because of the secretive methods used by these stock detectives it has been suggested that perhaps the cold-blooded nature of the Jones and Tisdale killings were the work of Tom Horn, a killer-for-sale who was also employed by the WSGA at that time. It is also clear that the Association detectives knew of would-be targets and that Canton in particular, if not guilty himself, was likely to have known Jones's and Tisdale's killer.

The Northern Wyoming Farmers and Stock Growers Association (NWFSGA) was founded on 21 November 1891 to represent small ranchers who opposed the Cheyenne-based cattle barons. Tensions continued to mount over the coming months as John Clay's associates accused Champion, an NWFSGA top hand, of organising independent round-ups of cattle belonging to WSGA members. In April 1892 the long-predicted action began when Frank Canton, still under suspicion of the Tisdale killings, was granted bail. The Cheyenne court set his bail bond at a staggering $30,000 which was met by some leading members of the WSGA. Canton's expert knowledge of the Johnson County 'rustlers' was vital to their plans and placed him at the centre of the forthcoming action.

On 5 April 1892 Major Wolcott, Billy Irvine, Canton and Tom Smith, the recruiter for the hired Texan gunmen, put into action their long-agreed plan for the 'cattlemen's invasion' of Johnson County. This involved a significant number of Scots by birth or descent. Scottish foremen and other employees of Scottish and British-owned companies were prominent, and certain 'rustlers' were also of Scots origin. One of these was the sheriff of Buffalo, who was high on the death list. For the first leg to Casper, 250 miles north west of Cheyenne, Wolcott's 'invaders' used a specially rigged-up Union Pacific train carrying twenty-five hired gunmen, nineteen local cattlemen, five stock detectives and six hand-picked observers and journalists.

The 'invaders' called themselves the Regulators and their death list of around seventy 'nominations' had been gathered from Stock Growers' members and approved by the Cheyenne executive. They disembarked and rode north to the KC Ranch, where they cornered Nate Champion and a fellow 'nominee', Nick Ray, who was fatally wounded when he left the cabin. He first crawled and was then dragged back inside. Champion scribbled an account of the ambush in his note book over his dying friend's body before the cabin was torched and he died in a hail of bullets whilst trying to escape.

Earlier in the day a cowboy called Jack Flagg, named at the top of the death list, had driven into the firing line by chance. He managed to escape the besiegers and raised the alarm in Buffalo, fifteen miles away. But Buffalo's Sheriff William Galispie 'Red' Angus, a leading 'nominee', counselled caution as he led a two hundred-strong posse. They were too late to save Nate Champion whom they found with a note pinned to his bloodstained body saying 'Cattle Thieves, Beware!' but they did find his sensational diary, which was quickly published in the *Cheyenne Daily Leader*, on 14 April. His blow-by-blow account of the siege ended:

> Well, they have just got through shelling the house again like hail. I heard them splitting wood. I guess they are going to fire the house tonight. I think I will make a break when night comes, if alive... Shooting again. I think they will fire the house this time... The house is all fired. Good-by, boys, if I never see you again. Nathan D Champion.

The posse pursued Wolcott's war-party to the TA Ranch, thirty miles nearer Buffalo. There they turned the tables by surrounding the Regulators there. For three days the siege continued. News of the Invaders' plight was eventually smuggled out and passed by wire to Cheyenne, political strings were pulled and US President Harrison became involved. The result was the dispatch of three troops of the 6th US Cavalry from nearby Fort McKinley. The Cavalry arrived in the nick of time to lift the siege and take the Regulators into protective custody. It was the stuff of future Western movies.

Another close associate of John Clay's was also involved in the 'invasion'. James T Craig, a member of the Western South Dakota Stock Growers Association, was a boyhood friend of Clay's in Scotland. Clay had put him in charge of the day-to-day management of the Western Ranch headquarters on the Belle Fourche River, across the State line but close to Johnson County. Craig had been a character witness and alibi for Frank Canton during the previous winter and was able to warn the Regulators ahead of the huge posse from Buffalo. This brought about their hasty retreat to the TA ranch. However, their wagons, loaded with ammunition and food, were later intercepted by Sheriff Red Angus's men and put to use against the besieged Regulators.

The aftermath was a political and judicial mess. Johnson

County and neighbouring ranching areas were in a state of fear. American 'white cap' vigilantism had apparently come to Wyoming. Naturally the local authorities wanted to try the 'white caps', as they called the Regulators, fifty of whom were transferred under military escort and kept in loose confinement at Cheyenne for their own safety. Meanwhile high-powered lawyers were engaged by the WSGA to ensure their release. This was eased by the lack of witnesses, since the trappers captured at the KC Ranch before Nick Ray was shot had been spirited out of the State. The cost of keeping the fifty Regulators as prisoners bankrupted Johnson County. Various revenge killings shortly followed and Wolcott was disgraced along with others for the use of running irons.

The Johnson County Invasion signalled the last hurrah for the open range ranching system in the Old West. It also curtailed crime. Consequently the cattle barons were forced to accept the need for fencing and winter fodder for their cattle and to allow the settlers to stay. Their Johnson County invasion had been modelled on the actions of Montana cattlemen a decade beforehand but by 1892 the frontier's closure was now an indisputable fact.

John Clay, who had been in Europe during the action (as he constantly reminded the world thereafter), later admitted that Wolcott had told him of a 'lynching bee' for Averill. He claimed, however, that having strongly advised against it, 'the matter left my mind.' On his return from Europe Clay presided over the WSGA annual meeting on 4 April, 1893. The ninety-nine members heard a long speech in which his subject-matter ranged from uncertain prospects in the cattle markets to the outcome of the Johnson County Invasion. His open sympathy with his associates was underlined by his concluding remarks:

I am not here to defend these parties. Technically, legally, they did wrong, but I consider it no mean privilege to stand in this prominent position today to say that I count every one of them a friend. Notwithstanding their errors of judgement, we respect them for their manliness... There will be a day of retribution, and the traitors in the camp and in the field will be winnowed like wheat from the chaff.[3]

The following year Clay was incensed by charges of complicity in the Invasion. The assault on his reputation came from Asa Mercer, the former editor of the Cheyenne-based North West Live Stock Journal which, since 1883, had been financed by stockmen like Clay. Mercer had played a distinguished part in the settlement of Washington Territory and in the founding of its University. He had written optimistic reports on the cattle trade even in the terrible winter of 1886-87. But in 1894, at the age of fifty-five, he turned against his former Republican friends, penning The Banditti of the Plains, or the Cattlemen's Invasion of Wyoming in 1892, a 'highly damaging story of that notorious episode'.

Clay's friends quickly suppressed Mercer's book and few copies remained in circulation. Mercer had earlier printed the confession of Idaho gunman George Dunning who had been recruited by WSGA official, Hiram Ijams, for the Invasion. The sensational revelations of the blood money on offer seemed to implicate prominent Wyoming citizens including the Governor. They helped swing the State elections in favour of Mercer's new-found friends in the Democratic Party.

Clay claimed to have been 'unconscious of any cattle war' when applying twenty years' hindsight. He reflected that it was a 'pretty bad business... and yet if you had lived in such times the critics of today would probably have been the performer of a faraway yesterday'. His conclusion was: 'In this world of complex conditions it is hard to define where law ends and individuality begins.' Pontius Pilate couldn't have put it better.

In a reprinted edition of Mercer's book published in 1954, a new introduction by William H Kitrell weighed up the Invasion of Johnson County:

> All of the cattle barons were not oppressors, nor were all the settlers rustlers, but there were enough of each to explain the crude measures used and make more tolerable the intolerance that resulted... under such circumstances, men are prone to take the law into their own hands. Tolerance and tenderness could not flourish under these conditions. I am willing to allow for violence and sudden death, on quick and sufficient provocation, but planned and deliberate murder, the bloody carrying out of lawless decrees, cannot be placed in this category.[4]

John Clay had been a big player in the troubled development of Wyoming. This Scottish cattle and land assessor, commission agent and financial middle-man is the classic example of a pragmatic businessman who made decisions and sought authorisation later. When cornered, he prevaricated over his borderline management practices. Picture him amongst his wealthy friends, wearing a pink dinner jacket with white tie and shirt (the attire dubbed a 'Hereford' because of its resemblance to the distinctive red and white colouring of that celebrated cattle breed). Often leading the singing as he stood by the grand piano in the opulent Cheyenne Club, he epitomised not only flamboyance and astute business sense but also the arrogance of power.

References

1. Lawrence Woods, *British Gentlemen in the West* (London, Robson Books, 1990).

2. R Winter, *The Oxford Book of the American West* (New York, OUP, 1994), chapter 'Animals and Enterprise'.

3. AS Mercer, *The Banditti of the Plains, or the Cattlemen's Invasion of Wyoming in 1892* (new edition Norman, University of Oklahoma Press, 1954), p 135.

4. William H Kitrell, forward to 1954 edition, *The Banditti of the Plains* (Norman, University of Oklahoma Press, 1954), p XLIV.

CHAPTER 11

Our Scotsman Out West – Murdo MacKenzie

THE PRAIRIE LAND AND Cattle Company was founded by Edinburgh investors in December 1880. By the following year it owned 117,000 acres of range land, eventually with blocks in south-east Colorado, north-east New Mexico and the Texas Panhandle. The first chairman, until his early death the following year, was the Earl of Airlie. The company had sprung from the Scottish American Investment Company which had already developed a successful mortgage business on the rapidly developing frontier. This consortium of business interests saw huge potential profits in cattle and they achieved these in its first few years of trading. By 1883 their return on investment exceeded 20 per cent.

Thereafter, drought and doubt raised difficult questions for the Edinburgh-based board. Drought on the Plains was a perennial problem, and doubts about the stock and level of calf production led, in 1885, to the appointment of Murdo Mackenzie as manager.

Mackenzie was born at Rathmore, Edderton in Easter Ross on 24 April 1850, the second of eleven children. His father was a small tenant farmer on the estate of Sir Charles Ross of Balnagowan, who owned over 50,000 acres. Murdo left Tain Royal Academy in 1869 destined for a land management career. He did a year's law apprenticeship, took a job in a Tain bank and then another as assistant factor on Balnagown estates. In

1876 he married a local lass, Isabella Stronach MacBain, and they had three sons and two daughters.

The Prairie Land and Cattle Company recruited Mackenzie on the strength of his land management skills and in 1885 he left Scotland with his family to set up home at Trinidad, Colorado. He supervised two ranching empires from that base, introducing a programme of enforced cutbacks in response to the disastrous winter of 1886-87. Although this action failed to regain the profitability previously achieved, the Prairie Company nevertheless traded successfully till the outbreak of World War One, when its shareholders were handsomely compensated. At the time of its liquidation the UK government was seeking to repatriate foreign investments to aid the war effort against Germany.

Mackenzie's career really took off when he accepted the post as manager of the giant Matador Land & Cattle Company. He held its top post from 1891 to 1911 and from 1922 to 1937.[1] His policy with the Matador was to order a reduction in herd numbers and to improve the quality of stock through the purchase of pure-bred Hereford bulls. Murdo developed the feeding of mature steers on northern ranges after a search for emergency grazings to supplement the drought-hit, home range grass. When short leases failed in Texas, a twin-track strategy was pursued. For several years the quality Matador product was displayed to potential buyers on fresh Kansas grass. However, the Kansas experiment cost more than was acceptable to the Dundee board. Thereafter, the second approach was to ship two-year old cattle to winter on northern grass for another two years, proving the key to MacKenzie's success. This aimed at gaining top prices in the Chicago markets and involved a deal with another of the web of Scottish cattle companies, Western Ranches, whose boss was none other than John Clay.

The Clay–Mackenzie relationship began with a chance conversation in Edinburgh between John Clay and the Matador Company secretary, Alexander Mackay. A business deal ensued between the Mackenzie and Clay Western Ranches, and from 1892 onwards the range on the Belle Fourche in Wyoming and South Dakota was offered at $1 per cow per year. Around 2,000 Matador two-year olds were trailed to the Belle Fourche country in the first year in a drive of over ten weeks duration. Thereafter they were carried by train from Clarendon, Texas to Orin, Wyoming and driven to Western Ranches land in three weeks.[2]

The Clay–Mackenzie relationship was characterised by constantly sparring over aspects of the agreed contract. Clay sought preference for his Chicago livestock commission business in handling the sale of finished Matador stock. Mackenzie's bosses agreed to this only if the service they first received from Clay, Robinson & Co. was maintained. For several years arguments peppered their dialogue about mixing herds and stray stock. There were also unanticipated costs to the Matador after some cattle were marketed by mistake by Western Ranches.

Mackenzie's misgivings about the looseness of the contract came to a head over Clay's refusal to accept liability for delivering the same cattle back to Matador hands after their grazing in Belle Fourche. Clay's interests called for a cap on Matador cattle numbers to 6,000 on the Belle Fourche range. An increase in annual rent to $1.125 was then demanded 3. Their deal ended in 1904. Western Ranches trade had been trading mainly from leased public lands. Homesteaders' claims were encroaching on Clay's business and rumours that it might cease trading prompted Mackenzie to seek larger grazings for rent in the north, whilst considering the purchase of new pastures in Texas. This twin track approach by the Matador lasted until 1928.

Nevertheless Murdo Mackenzie had won praise from his board in Dundee by proving that Texas-born two-year-old cattle wintered twice on northern grass would bring top prices. The Matador cattle won prizes for improved yearlings in the Chicago International Livestock Show in 1902, in Chicago and Kansas City in 1908; and in the Grand Championship Award at Chicago in 1911.[4] This saved the company from unstable market conditions during these critical years.

The value of good northern grass was fully exploited through successive extensive leases. These included the Cheyenne River Indian Reservation, South Dakota from 1904-14; 50,000 acres near Swift Current on the Saskatchewan River, Assiniboia, Canada from 1905-21; at Fort Belknap, on the Gros Ventre and Assiniboine Indian Reservation, Montana from 1913-28; and at Pine Ridge Sioux Reservation from 1921-26. Thereafter, in a much changed business climate[5], the firm concentrated on its Alamositas and Matador Divisions in Texas until 1951. One memento of the Matador's first lease in South Dakota is commemorated by a historical marker stating:

> Mighty few towns have one of them hi-faluting, swank Rolls-Royce type of hyphenated names. In 1904, Murdo Mackenzie, head of the Matador brand, with herds from Mexico to Canada, shipped train-load after trainload of Texas steers to Evarts to graze on good Dakota grass on the Standing Rock Reservation and a grateful railroad named a town for Murdo.[6]

As president of the American National Livestock Association from 1904 to 1911, Mackenzie gained great kudos. Despite the Matador board warning him not to incur extra expense, he led the campaign for the fair pricing of livestock rail transport. Having often thwarted the tyranny of the railroad company's pricing policies in shipping his two-year olds to northern grass-lands, he provided the American Congressional Committee with telling information on Interstate Trade. Not only had freight rates had been unfairly increased but the service had also become much poorer in the period from 1898 to 1904. This eventually led to the passage of the Hepburn Act of 1906 and brought compliments to Murdo Mackenzie as 'the most influential of western cattlemen' from the Wild West-loving President, Theodore Roosevelt. A sympathiser with Roosevelt's policy of regulating the use of the public domain, Mackenzie was appropriately appointed to the National Conservation Commission in 1908.[7]

1909 brought loss and tragedy to the MacKenzie's business and family life. Arthur Ligertwood, superintendent of the Matador Division and a Mackenzie associate for twenty years, resigned his post much to Murdo Mackenzie's dismay. And in the winter of that year his son Dode, who was boss of the company's Dakota Division, was shot dead in a sensational bar room brawl in Le Beau, South Dakota.[8] The barman Bud Stephens was an ex-Matador cowhand who was drunkenly challenged by Dode MacKenzie and was later acquitted. One shot killed his old boss while Dode's gun was later found to be empty, having had no ammunition loaded for a very long time.[9] Incidentally the bar owner was the infamous Phil DuFran, spy for the Invaders in Johnson County, Wyoming, back in 1892.

Dode's father got on with business as usual and travelled to Scotland in January 1910 to attend the company's AGM in Dundee. Whether these blows made him decide to resign from the Matador is not known. But after a meeting in 1911 in Denver he was persuaded by Scottish financier Percival Farquhar to accept the challenge to head the Brazil Land, Cattle and Packing Company based in Sao Paolo. His resignation was accepted with deep regret by the Matador board and his recommendation of a successor was accepted. His nephew John MacBain served as manager from Denver, Colorado till his sudden death in 1922. Mackenzie and family sailed to Sao Paolo in 1912 where he acquired millions of acres of grazing and ran a stock of 300,000 head for Percival Farquhar's new venture. Mackenzie's prestige attracted hundreds of applicants for jobs on the Brazilian project. Several key Matador men including his two remaining sons John and Alex joined him. The business was highly profitable until the post war slump. In 1918 MacKenzie returned to the USA having completed his stint in Brazil. He was immediately elected to the board of directors of the Matador Company.

On John MacBain's death, Mackenzie agreed to take over his old job and served the company as American manager till 1936. He remained shy of publicity, unlike John Clay, but was a highly successful cattleman on a huge and sustained scale. He never carried a gun despite the wild times he worked in, though the company's accounts show they used range detectives to root out rustlers. Two known hard cases named Higgins and Standifer, employed by the Matador, are thought to have shot or driven off likely rustlers, but themselves came to blows in 1904.[10]

Deeply loyal to his employers throughout his career, Murdo Mackenzie expected the same of all Matador employees. He banned drinking and gambling on the range and refused to tolerate disobedience from employees. Yet he had a sociable home life frequently playing his fiddle for dances, and was a humorous, hospitable father and friend. His recreations involved raising and riding fine horses and he became a master of sports fishing. Mackenzie gained a prestigious directorship of the Denver Branch of the Federal Reserve Bank in 1923. He held the post till 1935, two years before his death in Denver.

The Matador Company, which he managed for thirty-four years, was itself the longest lived of the foreign-based cattle enterprises in the USA. In some years it failed to pay dividends to its shareholders, but for many other years steady returns were gained, albeit at lower levels of profitability than British cattle investments in Argentina and Uruguay in the same period. A former trainee accountant in Dundee, Fred Sherriff, recalled that just before the start of the Second World War the partners of Mackay, Irons & Co. regularly travelled to Texas to review the annual balance sheet. The longevity of the Matador is a testament to sound business skills in a long Scottish tradition.

The Matador's liquidation in 1951 came about with an offer from Lazard Bros. of London who were seeking land in Texas for oil exploration. With a major oil strike near to Matador land the shares were sold at thirty times the original price, not including inflation. 'The Scottish people, as a nation, profited on investment in the American cattle business on a long term basis'[11] and Murdo Mackenzie, son of a small farmer from Easter Ross, had brought the steady, enlightened management needed to meet the demands of the huge cattle companies out West.

References

1. *Dictionary of American Biography.*

2. WM Pearce, *The Matador Land and Cattle Company* (Norman, University of Oklahoma Press, 1964), p 46.

3. Pearce, p 76.

4. Pearce, p 112.

5. Pearce, p113, (sketch map of approximate locations of major ranges used by Matador Company).

6. Brevet's *South Dakota Historical Markers* (South Dakota 1974), The marker is located on Main Street in Murdo, SD.

7. *Dictionary of American Biography.*

8. Pearce, p 127.

9. Mari Sandoz, *The Cattlemen*, From the Rio Grande across the Far Marias (Lincoln, University of Nebraska, reprint 1978), pp 468-9.

10. Sandoz, pp 421-4.

11. W Turrentine Jackson, *The Enterprising Scot, Investors in the American West after 1873* (Edinburgh, Edinburgh University Press, 1968), p 138.

CHAPTER 12

Scot in a Western Saddle – RB Cunninghame Graham

UNLIKE JOHN CLAY AND Murdo MacKenzie, Robert Bontine Cunninghame Graham was not a successful rancher, although he did try to set up business in South Texas in 1880, in the midst of the cattle investment boom. He is remembered as a traveller and writer who described his experiences and observations on the Western scene both in fictional and factual form. His insights into the fate of the winners and losers tell us much about frontier life. A fine horseman, taught by Argentinean gauchos, he captured the full flavour of cattle and horse ranching and gave these themes full expression in his short stories.

Cunninghame Graham first experienced the gaucho life on the Argentine and Uruguayan pampas as a teenager. An interesting family connection brought this about. He hated school life at Harrow, and by the time he had reached the age of seventeen his mother was worried about his future. (His father, chronically ill due to a blow on the head received on army duties in Ireland, was confined to a remote private house in Dumfries-shire). It was one of Robert's aunts, the Countess of Airlie, who suggested that he get a sense of adventure by joining two of her cousins on an estancia in Argentina.

Robert reached South America by emigrant ship after a passage during which he was chronically seasick. On arrival, he found his Airlie cousins were hopeless alcoholics and the condition of their estancia in a parlous state. So he left with a visiting drover, and was caught up in a revolutionary army that had been scouring the pampas for horses to steal, although he did little actual fighting. He spent the best part of the next seven years in the saddle in a number of South American countries, becoming an accomplished rider and drover. This experience marked his whole outlook thereafter and confirmed his love for the Hispanic world and particularly the peoples living at the edge of civilisation such as the half-Indian, half-Spanish gauchos. His own family had Spanish blood in its veins and he developed a deep rapport with native peoples oppressed by imperialists.

Later, he tried to give voice to the causes of underdogs by sitting as a radical Liberal in the House of Commons. Right at the heart of the British Empire, he exposed, with intelligence and wit, the excesses of business interests let loose on the colonies. A proto-socialist from a radical family, he sat from 1886 to 1892 as MP for the mining constituency of North Lanarkshire. He argued for an end to the land monopoly of the rich – legislation that would, if achieved, remove his own inheritance of several thousand acres at Gartmore in Stirlingshire.

The sight of Highland drovers passing by his family home at Gartmore on the edge of the Trossachs had fascinated the young Cunninghame Graham. As Lowland Scots lairds, his Graham ancestors had often come to blows with their predatory Highland neighbours, the MacGregors, who were expert blackmailers and cattle thieves. He appreciated what it was like to live on frontiers before he arrived on the pampas of South America and later the Great Plains of North America.

At the age of twenty-seven, with Gabriela, his young wife of six months, Robert sailed to New Orleans intent on breeding mules near Brownsville on the Texas-Mexico border. Their stay there lasted a fortnight, for what they found was an intolerably violent society. Moving 150 miles up the coast to Corpus Christi, they bought a hundred acres of land but soon encountered a similar situation. Writing home to his mother he noted:

> Words are inadequate for the citizens about here, their meanness, hypocrisy and assassination, being beyond all bounds. I don't believe in Italy in the Middle Ages there was so much assassination as there is in Texas today. Every day there is one or two, such a thing as a fair fight is unknown, & if you enquire how so 'n' so was killed, I guess Sir waited for him in the Chaparral & shot him in the back Sir.[1]

Robert and Gabriela were soon on the move again, to San Antonio, with its old Spanish houses and famous ruins of the Alamo mission, where 200 Texans had been massacred in 1836 by Santa Anna's Mexican Army. The slogan 'Remember the Alamo!' had thereafter been coined by Texans who defeated the Mexicans forty-six days later to win de facto independence for the fledgling Texas Republic. The aftermath in human terms was anything but peaceful. The Spanish-American ranch traditions of the area had attracted Anglo-American settlers where the resident mestizo cowboys taught the Anglos how to ranch. Cunninghame Graham was later dubbed Don Roberto by people who likened his support for allegedly lost causes to Don Quixote's in Cervantes' famous seventeenth century novel. Many terms the cowboys used were corrupted or borrowed Spanish words (e.g. lasso, from the Spanish *lazo*, for roping steers and horses), and he made reference to this:

> The genesis of the lazo from Andalucia to Mexico and thence to Texas, to California and the north-west, is curious enough, and an additional proof that in the first instance all the cowboy's lore reached them, through Mexico, from Spain.[2]

In other words, a much older Mexican civilisation was rudely shattered by United States-backed businessmen intent on carving out cattle empires in Texas. Besides the American-Hispanic hostility, the real underclass was the local Indian tribes. Cunninghame Graham wrote in a letter home that 'the English-speakers oppressed the Spanish-speakers and the Indians, the Spanish-speakers oppressed the Indians, the Indians terrorised whom they could.'

The Cunninghame Grahams decided on more adventure and set out on a hazardous two-month long trip to Mexico City. Robert's letters told of being armed with a sword, knife, pistol and Winchester carbine. He tied his horse's reins to his head as he slept for fear of attack or treachery by the Mexican guides or by Indian raiding parties, of whom much news was heard along the way. They spent two months in Mexico City and in their leisure time saw the sights, amongst which were eight captured Mescalero Apache, exhibited behind bars in the Chapultepec fortress. During their return journey to Texas the Cunninghame Grahams heard further news that the Apaches had overpowered their guards and escaped. Six warriors, a woman and child proceeded to cause much panic over a distance of eight hundred miles before they were eventually hunted down and killed. Cunninghame Graham later met a Texan rancher and his five Mexican cowboys who had shot the last of that bedraggled band – a man, woman and boy – whose escape had terrorised so much of northern Mexico. These half-starved, Indian fugitives left a big impression on Don Roberto and were commemorated in his story *A Hegira* in 1900.

From 1879 to 1886 various Apache bands caused havoc in Texas, New Mexico and south of the border in Chihuahua and Sonora. They made huge circling raids that tied up units of the

US Cavalry, the Mexican local police, the rurales, and eventually Mexican regular forces. Geronimo, Juh, Victorio and Nana combined to terrorise the ranching communities until official co-operation sanctioned by Mexican and US governments hunted down and massacred those they could while others were corralled in Indian Reservations, such as San Carlos, by US General George Crook.[3] It was the Cunninghame Graham's misfortune to attempt ranching during the height of this unsettled period. Reaching Texas once more, Robert set up in partnership with a Mexican-Greek in a location 'a week's hard ride from San Antonio'. His luck failed again for, during his partner's absence, Mimbres Indians, probably led by their war chief Victorio, razed the ranch and stole the stock. In the spring of 1881 Robert and Gabriela left for home in Scotland, £2,000 in debt from their failed investments and adventures in Mexico and Texas. Their return was spurred by the receipt of news of his father's failing health. Robert himself was already suffering from inflammation of a kidney having been kicked by a horse, and subsequently endured a bout of malaria.

But Don Roberto never lost interest in the American West. A politician and writer, he carried on a polemical commentary on the clash between the colonisers and the colonised. He found the various native populations more sinned against than sinning and eloquently advocated their cause. In three letters to London newspapers in 1890 he explored the plight of the Sioux peoples who were consigned to various reservations in Montana and South Dakota, as many are to the present day. Reservation life bred disease, alcoholism and numerous revolts. The successful attempts by the Washington government to defraud the Sioux of their Montana reservation land and force them into smaller, separated areas, led to support for the millenarian Ghost Dance movement, invented by a Paiute messiah, Wovoka. The medicine man hoped it would deliver the tribes from their tribulations:

> If the Indians refrained from violence. And if they were virtuous and performed the proper ritual dance - the Ghost Dance - they could hasten the coming of the New World, which would cover the old and push the white man into the sea.

By mid-1890 religious revival frenzy had taken hold among the Sioux clans. When a sceptical Sitting Bull allowed his Huncpapa clan to be taught the Ghost Dance, the white authorities panicked. The great chief's arrest and violent death on 15 December led directly to a conjoining of the remaining Huncpapa and Miniconjou under Chief Big Foot. They gathered at Standing Rock on the Cheyenne River intent on seeking Chief Red Cloud's protection on the Pine Ridge Reservation. However Big Foot's band was confronted and massacred on 29 December 1890 at Wounded Knee by three US regiments, including units of the Seventh Cavalry.

Writing within days of Wounded Knee, Cunninghame Graham raged in the London newspaper *The Daily Graphic*:

> I wonder if the British public realises that it is the Sioux themselves who are the Ghosts dancing. Ghosts of a primeval race. Ghosts of ghosts, who for three hundred years, through no crimes committed by themselves, except being born, if it be not a crime to love better the rustle of the grass than the shrieking of the engine, have suffered their long purgatory. Ghosts who were men. The buffalo have gone first, their bones whitening in long lines on the prairie, the elk have retired into the extreme deserts of Oregon, the beaver is exterminated to make jackets for the sweater's wife. The Indian must go next and why not, pray? Is he not of less value than the other three?

Let him make place for better things; for the drinking shop, for the speculator, for the tin church.

He stood against the free-for-all exploitation of native lands and resources justified by the tenets of Social Darwinism, and underpinned by imperial conquest. In his maiden speech in Parliament in 1886, he argued that it beggared the poor at home and exterminated native peoples abroad; again and again he condemned the activities of exploitative cattle, timber and mineral companies and crooked traders. Other American examples concerned the potential exploitation of the settlers themselves. When local Dakota politicians were elected on a policy to wipe out the Indians, Cunninghame Graham prophesied that:

those who are loudest now, for the final extermination of the Sioux fail to grasp that when Dakota is all settled they themselves will in the main become dependent on the capitalists as the Indians now are on the US Government, and that the precedent of rigorous measures with the starving Indians will be used against them.

Cowboy life was by any measure lonely, harsh, and dangerous. Anglo-American employers first learned the cattle ranching skills from the Mexicans and later employed Blacks to be cowboys, first as slaves then as cheap labour. Reliable estimates show the Texas trail drives employed 25 per cent Hispanic cowboys and 12 per cent Blacks. They would, of course, have been paid much less than Anglos. While many British aristocrats became cattlemen, few Anglos stuck the weary life in the saddle, the low pay, the lonely sod huts and the isolation. It is said that only a third of cowboys rode a trail drive for a second time. Further deterioration in conditions came with the ending of the open range, when barbed wire was erected by these very cowhands to protect the much reduced, but ultimately much more valuable, herds of cross-bred beef cattle in the lean years after 1887.

A foretaste came in 1883 when the Panhandle Stock Growers Association, led by Charles Goodnight, took on and broke a strike by cowpunchers for $50 a month. Strikers were blacklisted and Hispanics and Blacks were employed respectively at two third and a half of the $25 salary that the Whites had disputed. Itinerant Scots, emigrating from grinding poverty back home, sought cowhand and shepherding jobs out West. But their initial sense of adventure may well have been disappointed by the reality that had already shattered the dreams of so many young men who sought their fortune out West in the years immediately after the American Civil War.

Due to Anglo racism, Black and Hispanic cowboys seldom reached more exalted posts than camp cook. Indeed, by the late 1880s it was almost impossible for small ranchers to gain a foothold on the bottom rung of a ranch-owning career ladder. As the Earl of Airlie and others predicted, only big companies survived in the cattle business. Charles Goodnight's JA, the King Ranch, the Matador, the Prairie and Western ranches proved the point.

Despite his socialist zeal, Cunninghame Graham, dubbed the 'cowboy dandy' by the *Times*, was dispirited about the prospects of toppling the system at home by means of the Independent Labour Party, which he helped Keir Hardie to found in 1888. Though he continued to back Hardie's work and the international perspective of the ILP, his views were increasingly expressed as an individual commentator keeping a brave flag flying for the underdog throughout his life. The failure of European workers to stop the First World War led him to volunteer for the cavalry. Due to his age he was sent to Argentina to select horses for use on the western Front.

Over the course of his long life, he had observed Scots drovers, had learned to ride like a gaucho, and remained an excellent horseman. In this guise he wrote a highly informative introduction to an account by artist Charles Simpson in sketches of the Great International Contest in 1924. The contest, an American rodeo brought to Wembley Stadium, London in 1924, that included wild bronco riding, steer roping and bull dogging as well as western-style horse races. Dismissing the ill-informed critics who had alleged cruelty, he noted that the charges had been dispelled by the Society for the Protection of Animals. Why was it that those who were ignorant of the rodeo felt they could 'enjoy the latitude of speech rarely vouchsafed them' to attack this new form of sport?

Don Roberto recalled that in 1891 and 1904, when Buffalo Bill's Wild West Show reached Britain, he had brought Indians and buffaloes to display the life on the frontier. 'Few understood that his great show was in reality a panorama of a life just passing, in which he and his comrades had borne considerable roles.' The international rodeo was a celebration of a sport that had developed from the work of cowboys who still provided much of the beef consumed in Europe. Compared his own 1880 cattle venture in West Texas in free ranging days, ranching had become highly organised. It was the work of men like MacKenzie and Clay who had consolidated the industry into its modern industrialised form and cowboys of Anglo, Hispanic and Black roots who had done the hard work.

Cunninghame Graham's writing on feats of horsemanship, South American dictators and the demise of native peoples continued into the 1930s. He was also consistent in his views at home where he championed the cause of Home Rule for Scotland. He helped co-found the National Party of Scotland in 1928 and became the president of its successor, the Scottish National Party, in 1934. It crowned a life's effort to achieve Scotland's social, cultural and economic independence from the British Empire. In a last journey, he sailed in 1936 to Buenos Aires where he was greeted with great acclaim for his much-loved portrayal of life on the pampas in the early days of the Argentine nation. There he died and his body was returned to Scotland on the steamer in which he had planned to travel back home. He was buried alongside his wife Gabriela, whose grave he had dug years before, on the Isle of Inchmahome, Lake of Mentieth, in Stirlingshire.

References

1. Cedric Watts and Laurence Davies, *Cunninghame Graham: A Critical Biography* (Cambridge, CUP, 1979), p 43.

2. Charles Simpson, with an introduction by RB Cunninghame Graham, *El Rodeo* (London, John Lane, The Bodley Head, 1925), p 17.

3. Frank McLynn, *Villa and Zapata*, a *Biography of the Mexican Revolution* (London, Pimlico, 2001) pp 54-8, contains a succinct summary of the Apache campaigns.

CHAPTER 13

America for the Americans – Scotland for the Scots?

'BRITISHERS WHO ACQUIRED LAND in the West have antagonised the homesteader, the democrat and the American' claimed a leading US politician in the 1880s at the height of the inward investment in Texas cattle. At that time, the US Interior Department estimated that twenty-nine foreign-owned companies owned twenty million US acres. US Interior Secretary Teller claimed cattlemen's fences riled settlers and were a deplorable enclosure of public land. Of course, Americans were far more involved in illegal fencing operations than aliens were, but it was the latter who received such politically-generated publicity. In 1884 the cry 'America for Americans' was the rally of Republican Presidential candidate JG Blaine who declared, 'While railroad granted lands are safest for aliens to invest in, homestead, desert [prairie] and timber land laws are being bent to amass land for big purchasers.' Though he was defeated by Democrat Grover Cleveland, a law was pushed through Congress to ban illegal fencing of public lands and within a few months the ranchers' barbed wire had been cleared from the Arapaho and Cherokee Territories. From London, the business journal *The Economist* warned, 'our land speculators cannot be surprised at the wrath descending on their heads when they fly in the face of laws intended to protect settlers'. The Prairie Land and Cattle Co. complied by abandoning 200,000 acres in Colorado rather than contest the issue with Land Office officials.

The effect of the new law reduced the rights of aliens, effectively absentee landlords, to own American land. The Public Land Commission denounced the practice as 'a system of landlordism incompatible with the best interests and free institutions of the United States'. The 1887 Act limited the size of foreign individuals and corporations acquisitions of US real estate in future, except by inheritance or as payment for debts. Corporations which had 20 per cent or more of their share capital held by aliens were prohibited from making further purchases and were restricted to a maximum of 5,000 acres property holding. These restrictions did not greatly affect companies, like Matador, which rented land in Texas, where the rental income and sale of state land was earmarked for funding education. However, mining investment in various states and territories was adversely affected. This ceased to be an issue when the era of quick profits collapsed with the free range on the frontier.

Meanwhile, in Britain Gladstone's short-lived third administration had been torn apart in June 1886 over Home Rule for Ireland. Only one substantial piece of legislation was passed - the Crofters' Holdings (Scotland) Act. While it gave legal redress for small landholders and security of tenure for crofters, it did not outlaw absentee landlords. It did not break up the pattern of land use and ownership that, in 1873, saw four-fifths of Scotland's nineteen million acres of land owned by just six hundred and fifty individuals; a mere 118 people owned one half of Scotland. It is interesting to reflect that in 1995, half of Scotland was still owned by only 608 people; indeed Scotland still suffers the most concentrated pattern of land-holding in Europe.[1] Change of ownership did take place, but rarely over much of the major holdings. One example in the Highlands shows the Duke of Sutherland owned over one million acres in 1873; his descendant the Countess of Sutherland, today owns 80,000 acres. Most of the balance was sold to other large-scale shooting estates such as the 95,100 acres owned by the trustees of the Duke of Westminster.

During the nineteenth century a new breed of landowners began to replace the clan chiefs. Urban industrialists and commercial speculators invested in fashionable shooting estates, and rich British subjects with land and cattle interests in the American West often rented or owned shooting estates in the Scottish Highlands. One example is Sir Dudley Coutts Marjoribanks, who bought the 20,000-acre Guisachan estate, Inverness-shire from the chief of the Chisholm clan in 1853. The Marjoribanks were a family of small landowners and lawyers near Edinburgh till one member made a fortune in the East Indies Co. in 1795 and bought a partnership in Coutts Bank. Sir Dudley was raised to the peerage as Baron Tweedmouth in 1866.[2]

As a partner in Coutts Bank, in 1883 he became a leading investor in the Rocking Chair Ranch syndicate with a cattle business operating south-east of the Texas Panhandle. Consequently his sons were sent out West. His youngest son, Archibald John, went to Texas as co-manager of the ranch, demanding, much to their annoyance, that he be addressed as 'sir' by his 'cow servants'! Archibald's brother imported pure-bred Aberdeen Angus cattle from his mother's herd to improve the stock on their Dakota spread.

Guisachan Estate in Strath Glass, which Sir Dudley turned over to deer forest in 1857, was on the main drove route from north-west Scotland. He expanded his interests by renting deer forests from various surrounding shooting estates. These included Ceannacroc, Corrimony and Affric, where he built a beautiful shooting lodge in 1870.[3] They were the lands from which the Chisholm clansfolk had been cleared, some of whose descendants, like Jessie Chisholm, later made a large and successful impact in America.

From around 1880 till 1895, Walter Winnans (whose father had founded a US engineering dynasty) rented a string of shooting estates, from Kintail in the west to Strathglass in the east, totalling a staggering 200,000 acres. Winnans took the idea of exclusivity to new lengths, employing gamekeepers and watchers to keep intruders off the hill and restrict them to the drove roads and tracks. He rarely visited his shootings, but when he did his methods of slaughter and the quantity of deer and game killed were considered extreme, even by the profligate standards of the day. In 1888 he went to court in a dispute with his neighbour, Lord Tweedmouth, over access and boundaries. The Scottish Court of Session ruled against him declaring that the tracks from Tomich to Torgyle and from Tomich to Corrimony were rights of way. Three years earlier, Winnans had come off worst in another legal dispute, this time over a crofter's pet lamb. In June 1885 the Court of Session ruled that a pet lamb kept by Murchadh MacRae from Morvich had not been illegally grazing in the Kintail deer forest that the American sportsman rented from Sir James MacKenzie.

In the 1880s the plight of starving crofters and cottars caused outrage amongst various political groups, including those inspired by the American author of *Progress & Poverty*, Henry George. Though feted on his tour of Scotland, his Land Tax campaign gained surprisingly little support amongst the mass membership of the Highland Land League. In the midst of the political turmoil *The Times* reported in 1887: 'for the purposes of sport capitalists prefer to hire rather than to buy, while for the purposes of investment they mistrust the security which land offers in present circumstances in England.' 'Present circumstances' included an agricultural depression that hit England hardest and was induced largely by cheap imports of grain and beef from the colonies and the US. It also meant continued crofters' and cottars' land agitation in the Scottish Highlands that made shooting estates vulnerable to sabotage of their sport. Robert Cunninghame Graham MP, writing from prison, declared that it seemed 'Scotland was a free country, for a crofter to starve in, or for a deer to eat his crops in'.

Four Land League Members of Parliament were elected in 1885 and 1886. They mounted a long-term campaign against deer forests although the resulting Royal Commission in 1892 was indecisive. Only straitened economic conditions after World War One led to the reduction of the Scottish acreage preserved for game.

There are clear parallels between the behaviour of landed interests in the Highlands and the American West. The sportsmen of the Scottish Highlands went to great lengths to retain their exclusive use of vast acreage of each country. Strangely, some of the same people who owned shares in ranching companies were the very sportsmen in question.

In the present day, agitation for land reform has intensified with the establishment of a Scottish Parliament. Radical calls have been made for major changes in land tenure and management because so many estates are still owned by absentee landlords and overseas interests. This prompted a Dutch professor, Jan van der Ploag from the Agricultural University at Wageningen, to comment on BBC Scotland TV in 1995, 'it is curious how people treat land (in Scotland). Land is simply a commodity. This is Wild West capitalism. Elsewhere in Europe this is not the case. It makes Scotland a truly unique case.' Only now are the first serious moves being made to address the land reform issue free from interference by the House of Lords. Significantly, in its first year of operation the Scottish Parliament set in train the abolition of the feudal land owning system.

References

1. Andy Wightman, *Who Owns Scotland* (Edinburgh, Canongate, Edinburgh, 1996), pp 157-58.
2. Thomas Johnston, *Our Noble Families* (Glasgow, Forward, 1918), p 119.
3. Willie Orr, *Deer Forest, Landlords and Crofters* (Edinburgh, John Donald, 1982). Also A.E. Robertson, *Old Tracks – cross-country routes and 'Coffin Roads' in the North West Highlands* (Edinburgh, Scottish Rights of Way Society, 1941), p 16.

Were drovers and cowboys outcasts?

Life on any frontier is rough and ready. Drovers, cowboys, *vaqueros* and gauchos were regarded as wild and danger-ous by the authorities and the more settled communities in Scotland, the USA and Argentina. In the heyday of the Wild West, romantic dime novels and eventually fictional Western films built up the rugged figure of the strong, silent Anglo cowboy.

Jobs that involved travel outside the settled community were open to envy or suspicion. Robert Cunninghame Graham mused in his essay *Falkirk Tryst* that 'the Lowland ploughmen working in the fields looked at the drovers as a man accustomed to office work looks on a sailor as he passes by, with feelings oscillating between contempt and envy of his adventurous life.' Contrast the annual welcome afforded the drovers of old as they arrived in Highland glens to buy cattle. Their appearance signalled ceilidh time, before low prices were reluctantly agreed upon the morning after. The popular view of roustabouts on North Sea oilrigs has a similar ambiva-lence.

John Prebble suggested that drovers in olden times had been landless men, without clan allegiance or pride, except in quarrelsome drink. Perhaps he was influenced in part by Sir Walter Scott's 'Two Drovers'. In fact the clan gentry regularly organised the droving trade year, ensuring that the clansmen's yearly round included seasonal journeys to cattle Trysts. They certainly plied a rough and ready trade in which a one-to-one dealing system required both courage and rare skills. The celebrations after a successful sale at Falkirk could be as wild as in any Kansas cattle town.

Cowboys on the huge untamed grassland frontier lived a lonely life. The low pay endured by Anglos, Blacks, Mexicans and Indians, who were employed by cost-cutting ranchers, gave the trade a low status. Yet the cowboy was meant to face up to danger with 'no right of retreat'. Differences were expected to be settled with a well-aimed bullet. While the gaucho considered guns to be cowardly, preferring his façon – a two-foot long knife – Canada gained the reputation for being the Mild West where Mounties ensured that fewer guns were shot in anger. But the frontier mentality still prevailed.

CHAPTER 14

Emigrants and Migrants – Transferable Skills and Conflicts

SCOTLAND, PARTICULARLY THE Highlands and Islands, has had a mobile, migrant society for centuries. Travelling to find work in the south or abroad had been a harsh economic necessity. When opportunities to work in the USA and Canada were advertised, they became a highly sought destination for Scots of all levels of wealth, skill and ability. Many were able to work for Scottish-owned companies in North America.

The Hudson's Bay Company aimed at fur trading when it received its charter in 1670. After riding out fierce competition from the North West Company in 1838, it developed a general trade with the far-flung north-west of Canada which continues to the present day. With the accumulation of wealth from home manufacturing, the canny Scot, with some cash to spare, invested heavily in land mortgaging, mining, logging and ranching interests in the USA during the key decades at the end of the 19th century. Many families had members on both sides of the Atlantic. Seeking better times often led those from pastoral and rural backgrounds to gravitate west from initial landfalls in Cape Breton, Nova Scotia or the eastern states of America, where the lure of the ranching and the farming frontier beckoned.

Surveys in the 1990s of Canadian and US citizens show that Scots make up a significant population group in each country. Calculations place 4.8 per cent of Canadians and 4.4 per cent of Americans as of Scots descent. That makes Scots the fifth largest group in Canada and eighth largest in the USA. Of course, there are nearly ten times more US citizens than Canadian citizens, so Scots descendants are more numerous but spread more thinly across the US population. Their impact in both countries is recognised in industry, commerce, law and education. It is said that in western frontier towns you might regularly meet Scots shop keepers, lawyers and teachers.

Men of humble origin were to make it to the top. The Canadian Pacific Railroad magnates Donald Smith and George Stephen, born twenty-five miles apart in north-east Scotland, became Lord Strathcona and Lord Mount Stephen respectively. The route to Donald Smith's success came through perseverance climbing the greasy pole of Hudson's Bay Co. management, and investment in the Bank of Montreal. George Stephen, a gifted mathematics pupil, moved from textiles into finance, after a chance meeting in London with a relative from Canada who had succeeded in trading dry goods. Another example was Andrew Carnegie, the weaver's son from Dunfermline who made his fortune in US steel making. We have already seen, on a smaller scale, the success of entrepreneurs of the cattle trade such as farmers' sons Murdo MacKenzie and John Clay. There were many other Scots who also contributed to the long-term prosperity of the cattle business on both sides of the 49th parallel.

Family connections helped many Scots smooth their way to success. The Matador Co. boss Murdo MacKenzie was in the driving seat after 1891, allowing his sons John and David George 'Dode' and nephew John MacBain to play leading roles. Murdo's youngest son John succeeded his father in 1937 as manager. 'Dode' bossed the Dakota division for three years till he was shot in a saloon brawl on 1909. John MacBain served as accountant in Trinidad, Colorado in 1902 and became Murdo MacKenzie's successor from 1912-22.

A Dundee-based accountant, Alexander MacKay was appointed as the Matador Co. secretary in 1882 and became company chairman from 1915-36. He also controlled various other American investments for clients, sitting on the board of the Edinburgh-based syndicate who controlled the Western Ranche Co. His business contacts were invaluable. When the Matador board decided to explore the lease of grazing land in 1902 in Assiniboia (now part of Alberta and Saskatchewan), MacKay consulted his brother-in-law WA Burns. He was manager of the Bank of Nova Scotia in Ottawa, and would be a useful go-between as Burns was a friend of the Canadian Government land commissioner. Unfortunately the politics of an approaching Canadian general election intervened, slowing down the conclusion of a deal to rent 50,000 acres along the Saskatchewan River.

The mixed livestock and cropping system so typical of much of Scottish agriculture reached its peak in the beef and barley regime of Aberdeenshire where innovators such as William McCombie succeeded in promoting the Aberdeen Angus breed. This was close to the model of farming that adapted to conditions in the American Midwest. It was quite different from the free-range, free-grass Texas practice that had enjoyed three centuries' development in Mexico and on the Texas plains.

The Midwest model underpinned major farm settlement in the West after the end of the Civil War in 1865. Coincidentally, twenty years later, demands for higher-quality beef and the open range losses suffered through drought and blizzards ensured that improved breeds of cattle, winter feed and shelter would become universal practice east of the Rockies. Cattlemen in Wyoming, Montana and Alberta were quickest to adapt.

The US Canadian border is a complicated divide. North of the line its settlement was a predominantly English majority while south of the 49th parallel the majority was German. However, the great Missouri River system and the Great Plains themselves cross the border. Different national governments created parallel railroad services. The Northern Pacific Railroad in the USA drove through North Dakota and Montana while the Canadian Pacific Railway travelled through Saskatchewan and Alberta en route to British Columbia. Nevertheless, people moved very freely between both countries to make a living. In the 1850s a Canadian trader of Scots origin, Richard Grant, moved south to trade beef cattle with the emigrants on the Mullan Road at Deer Lodge, Montana. In 1862 his sons sold out to Conrad Kohrs, a former miner who developed Montana's biggest ranch of around one million acres with herds in four States and southern Canada.

Cross-border cattle rustling and the resale of stolen cattle and horses were endemic. Unlike the free-for-all to conquer the USA's Wild West, the Canadian government of Glasgow-born, Sir John A MacDonald worked more systematically. It agreed upon long-lasting Indian Treaties, surveyed the land and formed the North West Mounted Police in 1873 to build a network of forts to protect the future prairie provinces, before the bulk of settlers arrived.

American whisky traders fled before the Mounties' arrival from Fort Whoop-Up at Lethbridge, Alberta. The force kept Sitting Bull and his Lakota under surveillance and encouraged their peaceful return after they had crossed into Canada to dodge US forces following the Little Bighorn wipe-out in 1876 by the Sioux confederacy. Though the Mounties were to be reinforced, their huge beats and lack of reliable witnesses kept prosecutions to a minimum. The Mounties worked in co-operation with US peace officers, uncovering Canadian rustlers working with American partners from Montana and North Dakota.

Cowboys were often recruited across the border. DH Andrews, the Scots manager of Moreton Frewen's Powder River Ranch Co. in Wyoming recommended his top hand Ebb Johnson as a replacement for George Lane, another American cowboy who had risen to the top in Alberta. Johnson had successfully settled Frewen's cattle at Mosquito Creek, Alberta in 1886, so Andrews gave him a glowing reference for the Canadian North West Cattle Co. Johnson settled and married in Alberta in 1891. His best man was none other than his old Wyoming pal Harry Longbaugh, soon to be known as the Sundance Kid.

The Ottawa government had been encouraging ranching in the foothills of the Rockies during the 1880s by offering cheap leases of range-land south and west of Calgary. Cowboys from Texas to Montana joined recruits from eastern Canada, to develop the Alberta Foothills area. Representing the former was Peter Muirhead, born on a Michigan farm in 1856, the son of Scottish emigrants from Stirlingshire. He developed a lumber business and eventually, with backing from a partner, established himself in ranching by purchasing the Bar S ranch near Calgary in 1902. Of the Canadians, perhaps the most prominent were Senator Matthew Cochrane and Rod Macleay who built up the Rocking P Ranch on the Porcupine Hills north of Fort MacLeod, Alberta in the 1890s. The MacLeay family maintains a ranching operation there to this day. Such pioneers built a prosperous trade and soon Alberta's cattle industry rivalled that in neighbouring Montana. Albertan cattle were shipped to Eastern Canada via the Canadian Pacific Railroad and also to New England and the UK, which received 54,000 live beasts in 1884 and double that by 1900.

There has long been an understanding of the push and pull effects on migrants. For the young and ambitious a career out West could be a ladder to success. But as the frontier disappeared by around 1890, the concentration of wealth and power in big companies meant that starting out on your own was daunting. Scots cattle companies that succeeded were those with deep reserves, patience and a determination to invest in the long-term.

For those looking for work, circumstances had to be very straitened before considering work as hired hands on relatively low pay. For many young Highlanders and other agricultural workers caught in the depressing economic slump of the 1880s, the pull of the West was strong. However, push factors were also at work.

Conditions for small livestock farmers and crofters in the north of Scotland were precarious, due to poor harvests and lack of additional work. Even after the passing of Crofting Acts and some measures of land settlement following the Irish model, many were left seeking steady work. The British Empire and the USA beckoned. Such destinations also called to skilled industrial workers in the following decades. Weekly adverts appeared in local papers for cut-price passages offered by the Allan Line of Canada to place skilled men and families for work in the Canadian west.

The Highland predicament was linked to the sprawling sporting estates that by 1910 covered a third of the land area of the five Highland Counties. Consequently, sheep numbers continued to fall as the crofters' staple cash crop was hit. Scots lawyer Lord Kennedy, President of the Land Court, argued that if new laws were not enforced, land agitation and law breaking would again arise. He commented in his report for 1916:

> Unless the system of law and policy which places the preservation of deer and other game above the production of food, and which permits and encourages depopulation of the country for the pleasure of the wealthy of this and foreign nations is completely reversed, this decline of population will rapidly accelerate. The younger men will, in increasing numbers, emigrate to the colonies, rather than continue to bear the evils and abuses.[1]

Kennedy was merely echoing what Highlanders had known for over twenty years. By 1916 many thousands of Scots had already left to work overseas. A 1998 BBC Scotland television documentary, *The Emigrants – Na h' Eiltirich*, told the story of several generations of Lewis men and women, migrants from the same few villages, who were recruited to work for huge sheep companies in Patagonia. Agricultural colonies were set up on the Prairies as well as in Australia and New Zealand.

Contract workers were sought to service British companies across the globe. Young Highlanders were targeted for their agricultural skills; recruitment from Scottish west coast communities was a regular occurrence for over fifty years. Men from Achiltibuie often took work with sheep and cattle firms in the area around Billings, Montana. Others from Drumbuie and the Kyle of Lochalsh area were attracted to Miles City, a hundred miles downstream on the Yellowstone River. Recollections have been recorded of conducting the gathering of sheep, the roundup of cattle and their sale and despatch, entirely in Gaelic.

Many migrant crofters hoped to return home one day. Such

were the hopes of songwriter Murdo MacLean, a man from Coigach, who travelled from Wester Ross to work around Billings, Montana in 1900. He joined a group of shepherds and cattle hands from his home area who used a Billings hotel owned by Gaelic speakers as their base. MacLean eventually earned enough wages as a cowboy to return to Scotland and marry his sweetheart, where he fulfilled his plan, setting up a farm in the Black Isle, Easter Ross in 1907.[2]

But before this dream was achieved, MacLean composed a song in Gaelic for the entertainment of his fellow Celtic cowboys in the long Montana winters. *Mo Shoraidh Leis a'Coigich* – 'Farewell to Coigach'[3] praised the warmth of his childhood home, contrasting it poignantly with the lonely life experienced by ranch hands and shepherds in the Montana hills. In the days of his youth he had tended the sheep cropping the tips of the grass of Ben Mor Coigach; as a cowboy and herder at the foot of the Rocky Mountains he contended with wolves and cougars.

Verses bemoaned returning at nightfall, with his cattle in the relative safety of the fold, to the cold hearth in his Montana cabin. He used to hunt the prong-horned deer on the mountains with his neighbour, big Angus MacLeod, where they reminisced about the beautiful young girls of their youth 'who would not refuse our kisses'.

MacLeod harked back to the 'island of Scotland' that was 'above any place under the sun'. But unlike Murdo MacLean, he never fulfilled hopes of returning home; he settled in Ontario and farmed there for the rest of his life. For many others, returning home to join the British forces at the outbreak of war in 1914 meant an unmarked grave in Flanders and a name on some Highland war memorial.

To this day, there are close ties between families in Coigach and Montana; some continued to migrate from Scotland to Montana for shepherding and cowboy work till the 1930s. No doubt this situation has echoes in many areas of the Scottish Highlands and Islands, when the lack of opportunities at home forced many to travel far and wide in search of work.

References

1. Lord Kennedy, President of the Land Court, 1916 Annual Report, quoted as an appendix to JM MacDiarmid, *The Deer Forests – and how they are bleeding Scotland white* (Scottish Home Rule Association Glasgow, 1926).

2. From conversations and family documents. Discussed with Murdo MacLean's grand daughter, Mrs MacIver of 'Coigach', Cromlet, Invergordon, Ross-shire, 1999 and Iain MacLeod, Polbain, Achiltibuie, 2000 and 2001.

3. Valerie and Tom Bryan (compiled), *Ullapool – Music of Lochbroom and Coigach* (Strathkanaird, Drumrunie Press, 1988). Contains words and tune of *Mo Shoraidh Leis a'Coigich* (Farewell to Coigach) by Murdo MacLean.

CHAPTER 15

Drovers and Cowboys – Myths and Realities

THE TWENTY YEARS FOLLOWING 1867 were the heyday of the Western cowboy, as their numbers rose to around 25,000. Why then are cowboys far better known than the Scottish drovers – twenty years of Texas history compared with two thousand years of the European Celtic cattle culture? Examining the decline of an old culture and the rise of the new holds some clues, as does the real and imagined picture we can form of the links between them.

Hanoverian Britain experienced the start of the Industrial Revolution in the middle of the eighteenth century. Soon, water-powered mills gave way to steam, iron and steel. In the nineteenth century this would degrade areas rich in seams of coal and iron but enrich a new class of entrepreneurs who sold manufactured goods, setting an example to Europeans who colonised large 'empty' continents. From the beginning, the rich then invested abroad and bought wild land at home for recreation. Their ignorance of basic land-use principles destroyed pastoral landscapes in places as far apart as the Scottish Highlands and the American prairies. They pressurised the inhabitants of the Celtic fringe of Highland Scotland, Ireland and Wales to leave home and join the European emigrant tide on the American frontier.

Skills and crafts for sustaining life in these pastoral Celtic zones were deemed either quaint or plain backward. While

Victorian free-marketeers adored ancient Celtic lore, the Celts of their own day were treated as an inferior race who, in the minds of the dominant self-styled 'Saxon' or 'Teutonic' majority, reposed 'in the bosom of two graceless sisters – sluggishness and ignorance'.[1]

Unaccountably to these Victorian minds, the Highland peasants harboured a stubborn attachment to their materially poor homelands. On the vast pastures of the Americas, Australia and New Zealand, Celtic cowboys and stockmen adapted songs and music from home to ease their lonely lot. Their songs fused and transformed in the melting pot of American and Australian folk culture. Musically, the Scots and Irish had a big impact on American and Canadian musical life,[2] perhaps more than any other national groups they supplanted, apart from the Mexicans and the forgotten legion of Black cowboys.

The European exodus in the nineteenth century shifted a great energy from the Old World to the New. Scots, Irish and Norwegian emigrants contributed by far the biggest percentage shares of their national populations to this emigrant tide. Whether Gaels or Lowlanders, Scots had the basic education and skills that stood them in good stead. First it was country people, and then, later on in the century, skilled townsfolk who sought a better life, gravitating to the booming cities of the USA. What happened across the Atlantic often seemed far more meaningful and hopeful than much of the economic and social life back in Scotland and Ireland. What brought new confidence back home, late in the twentieth century, was the North Sea oil boom. This created a cultural, economic and political upsurge in Scotland while European Union membership saw Ireland blossom into a new Celtic Tiger economy.

As droving died out, the lore was largely lost until folklore students began to delve into the rich heritage and culture of Scotland's country dwellers. In the 1940s, folksong collectors for the Irish Folklore Commission, and in the 1950s from the Edinburgh-based School of Scottish Studies, uncovered a wealth of material.[3] Cultural and economic links were re-established with areas of Scots emigration, such as Cape Breton Island, Nova Scotia. These have recovered old Scottish tunes and step dances lost to Scotland for nearly two hundred years.[4] Life-giving cultural forces were unleashed in Scotland, as those links were re-forged.

It has been acknowledged by ethnomusicologists, such as American collector Francis James Child, in the domestic revival of folklore scholarship, that Scotland has the richest store of folksong of any country of its size in the world. Both Gaelic and Scots contribute to this amazing cultural legacy. When ARB Haldane started to chart the maze of former drove roads in the 1940s he was still able to select from a wealth of droving folklore from old men who remembered the Falkirk Tryst in its heyday. While his concerns were the physical business of droving, through his work we can reach into the treasure chest of Gaelic and Scots songs that revealed droving traditions to a far wider audience.

At the start of a new millennium the value of these old ways, both the routes and the roots, are interesting many more people. The building of a new Scotland involves understanding the realities of our past. The 20th century was dubbed the American century, and the central influence of American culture on our consciousness, including the legacy of the Wild West, remains strong. Despite the patina of glamour, the word 'cowboy' is in common usage in English as a derogatory term for unreliability or shoddiness. A 'cowboy builder' is tried in court, some 'cowboy tradesman' is accused in the papers; and 'cowboy breath' is a French description for halitosis. In North and South America, cowboys were treated as representative of a frontier mentality. In the US the myth of the rugged individualist Anglo cowboy became a national icon.

A fascination for Western films spans several generations of Scots and a strong working-class love of Country and Western music is another direct pointer to popular trans-Atlantic cultural influences. The Wild West theme crops up in children's songs, comic strips like 'Desperate Dan' in *The Dandy* (launched in 1937), and in Glasgow newspapers of the 1940s to the 1960s. It was epitomised by Bud Neill's cartoon characters Lobey Dosser, the wee cowboy sheriff of Calton Creek, and his sparring partner Rank Bajin who rode out on the Gallowgate frontier. A statue of Rank Bajin and Lobey on the back of Lobey's horse El Fideldo was erected by public subscription in Glasgow's Woodlands Road in 1992 as a posthumous tribute to his creator. More recently a Desperate Dan statue graces a central pedestrian area in Dundee.

Cowboy yarns were popular reading in many countries, Scotland included, for over a century. The 1840s produced the first dime novels romanticising Western adventure stories and the huge success of Owen Wister's 1902 novel *The Virginian* popularised the cowboy hero. Clearly they were writing history from the view of the winners, for therein can be found the myths that the Anglo-Americans were top hands. Mexicans, or 'greasers' as the Texans called Hispanics, are always portrayed as inferior, and Blacks are rarely mentioned. Zane Grey made a breakthrough to the big time in 1913 with his third Western novel *Riders of the Purple Sage*. From the first chapter a mixture of real and imagined images of the West were presented and sometimes created by people with little actual knowledge of reality. Even today the home grown, National Cowboy Hall of Fame based in Oklahoma City has little to say about the huge role of Hispanic and Black cowboys of the genre that it claims to celebrate.

The myth of the Wild West was developed by Buffalo Bill's Wild West Show that toured around America and Europe for over thirty years from the 1880s, making full use of the railways in America and Europe. Zane Grey's 1918 novel *The Roaring UP Trail* is a tale set around the construction of the Union Pacific Railroad. He quotes from Stevenson's *An Amateur Emigrant*, as a preface. Railways have had a major effect in droving history. Their arrival in northern Scotland and Wales ended the age-old droving trade; but when the railroad reached the Wild West it opened up the cattle markets of the eastern States and with the advent of fast ships US cattle producers were able to mount a serious challenge for European trade. In *An Amateur Emigrant* Stevenson gives his impressions of the 'deserts' of Kansas, Nebraska and Wyoming in the 1880s, seen from the emigrant train on which he crossed the continent. He captured the flavour of travel at that time on the iron horse:

> When I think how the railroad has been pushed through this unwatered wilderness and haunt of savage tribes; how at each stage of the construction, roaring impromptu cities, full of gold and lust and death, sprang up and then died away again, and are now but wayside stations in the desert; how in these uncouth places Chinese pirates worked side by side with border ruffians and broken men from Europe, gambling, drinking, quarrelling, and murdering like wolves; and then when I go on to remember that all this epical turmoil was conducted by gentlemen in frock-coats, with a view to nothing more extraordinary that a fortune and a subsequent visit to

Paris - it seems to me, as if this railway were the one typical achievement of the age in which we live, as if it brought together into one plot all the ends of the world and all the degrees of social rank, and offered to some great writer the busiest, the most extended, and the most varied subject for an enduring literary work. If it be romance, if it be contrast, if it be heroism that we require, what was Troy to this?

During the three months between November 1891 and February 1892, Bill Cody and company stayed in Dennistoun, Glasgow where approximately 700,000 people, i.e. around a sixth of the Scottish population, saw his shows. With its capacity audience of 8,000 per night in the covered hall of East End Industrial Exhibition, the impact was staggering. He returned to Scotland on another World Tour in 1904, much to the Scottish public's delight, playing as far north as Inverness.

Robert Cunninghame Graham, a friend of Bill Cody, felt the show cheapened the fast-disappearing frontier life of its cowboy, Indian and gaucho performers. Ironically Cody's own exploits were first embellished in Ned Buntline's story *Buffalo Bill: King of the Border Men* published in 1869, after which led Cody launched his stage show, *Scouts of the Prairie*. He briefly engaged Wild Bill Hickok, who proved an unreliable performer but he did borrow Hickok's idea of a spectacle involving live buffalo and tame Indians. Cody continued to tour his show in the years before the massacre of the 7th Cavalry at the Little Bighorn. Immediately following the event he returned to scouting and took 'the first scalp for Custer' on 17 July 1876. This feat became the publicity coup that boosted the box office draw of the Wild West Show on the strength of his growing fame. James Brisbin's *The Beef Bonanza* played up the economic lure of the West in 1881; a few years later, Buffalo Bill took his Wild

West show to conquer Europe. While many Scots were attracted economically, more travelled in imagination, through the lure of Western America.

Action-packed Westerns were an instant hit with early film audiences. The fledgling Hollywood movie industry fed the craving for vicarious frontier adventure with a stream of films following the success of *The Great Train Robbery* in 1903. Famous Westerners, including Bill Cody and Annie Oakley, were featured on film in the 1890s; and Wyatt Earp tried to sell his autobiography on the set of cowboy movies in Hollywood before his death in 1929. Charles Goodnight, the veteran cattleman, had seen the power of film and commissioned a documentary about the real life work of the cowboys. Where the all-action, fictitious West grabbed the public imagination, its realistic portrayals are all but forgotten.

Similarly romantic, distorted images of life in the Highlands also became dominant. But the eighteenth-century Gaelic poets Rob Donn and Duncan Ban MacIntyre portrayed the real Highlands. In the nineteenth century, General David Stewart of Garth wrote from first-hand knowledge of the dying Celtic culture as he observed it.[5] Stonemason Donald MacLeod of Strathnaver countered Harriet Beecher Stowe's *Sunny Memories of Sutherland* with the gloomy truth. Thomas Mulock, propagandist editor of the pro-crofter *Inverness Advertiser* and campaigning lawyer, Donald Ross, wrote in the 1840s and 1850s of the crofters' plight. The courageous, but impecunious, former exciseman John Murdoch laid down a manifesto for a fight back through land reform in his pioneering newspaper *The Highlander*, from 1873 to 1881. In the 1880s the fifty hearings of the Napier Commission held in churches and schools around the Highlands and Islands heard the unvarnished truth about the Clearances and the real reasons for the imposed destitution of crofters and cottars.

In 1981 John Keay drove thirty Highland cattle from Skye to Crieff in order to experience the feel of old time droving. During the journey he drew parallels between drovers and cowboys. He points out that the Highlands have suffered the same romanticisation as the Wild West. The Gaels, like the denizens of the London slums, had endured grinding poverty, 'but the Highlands had no Dickens; instead they got Scott and Landseer [who] ignored the sordid reality and glamorised the Highlands in precisely the same way as John Ford and John Wayne glamorised the American west'.[6]

Landseer painted nature, especially red deer, in misty Highland landscapes, which appealed to a wealthy, sporting clientele. In the USA artists such as Charles Russell and Frederick Remington caught the all-action, Western scene with raw energy from first hand experience. Russell's famous sketch, *Waiting for a Chinook*, shows a skin-and-bone steer, a survivor of the 1887 blizzards. It is a picture devoid of the romantic sentimentality that launched his public career. He befriended cowboys and Indians alike and chronicled the passing of the Old West on canvas and in sculpture from his base in Great Falls, Montana until his death in 1926.

Remington remained based in New York but his journeys gave him the raw material for many lucrative magazine illustrations. Like Theodore Roosevelt, who became Republican president of the USA in 1901, Remington held the belief that America was becoming over-civilised and corrupted by a 'foreign rabble'. He championed the simple virtues of rugged Western individualism that his paintings capture so well. But he turned his pen to a very questionable 'cowboy philosophy':

Jews, Injuns, Chinamen, Italians, Huns – the rubbish of the Earth I hate – I've got some Winchesters and when the massacring begins, I can get my share of 'em, and what's more, I will... Our race is full of sentiment. We invite the risins, the scourins, and the Devil's lavings to come to us and be men – something they haven't been, most of them, these hundreds of years...[7]

His extremism, even in such hard-nosed times was exceptional, but it also sums up a major strand of aggressive, Anglo-American capitalist thinking whose focus on 'the material interest' inspired Joseph Conrad's famous novel *Nostromo* (1904), a study of American imperialism in the fictional South American republic of Costaguana.

Big-league Hollywood film directors often produced films that romanticised Western tradition. However, John Ford's view of the West could be far from glamorous, despite his patriotic conservatism and recourse to slapstick as light relief. His series of cavalry films showed a frontier tamed by ordinary people embodying the idea of white American 'manifest destiny'. But one of his later films echoed the changing values of America at the time of the Civil Rights movement. Cheyenne Autumn (1964) charts the tragic flight of 286 Cheyenne men, women and children, pursued by the US cavalry from a barren Oklahoma reservation to their native Yellowstone country, 1,800 miles away.

Eight years earlier in *The Searchers* (1956) Ford brilliantly realised the psychological possibilities of the character Ethan Edwards, an embittered Confederate veteran. Ethan, played by John Wayne, returned some years after the war to his brother's west Texas homestead, from where he embarked on a five-year search for his two nieces after they are captured in a Comanche raid. It emerges that Edwards is driven by a murderous racism, determined to hunt down and kill his surviving niece, Debbie, because she has turned Comanche. In the final classic scene he is redeemed by sweeping her up in his arms; yet on their home-coming, he is symbolically excluded from normal family life by the ranch door shutting him out as he walks away into the desert. These classic movie scenes explore a motif that goes to the heart of the American conquest of the frontier and its civil-isation by family and community life.

The Searchers, based on a novel of the same name by Alan le May, has a different ending. It gives Edwards' companion on the search, Martin Pauley, an orphan, and part-Indian, the chance to save Debbie. Le May dedicates his work to his own grandfather, one of the many settlers who died trying to 'tame' the Plains, leaving a widow and three children under seven years old. His preface praised the grit of the early Texas settlers:

> ... these people had a kind of courage that may be the finest gift of man; the courage of those who simply keep on, and on, doing the next thing, far beyond all reasonable endurance, seldom thinking of themselves as martyred, and never thinking of themselves as brave.[8]

American movies have revealed a great variety of views on its history whereas Scotland, a tiny country by comparison, has yet to fully explore some of the major changes in its society. Liam Neeson's *Rob Roy* captured the essence of the Jacobite drover's predicament in the early eighteenth century, but no one has yet tackled the drama of a great Highland drove or of the Highland Clearances and subsequent diaspora, nor of the struggles of the Land League. Hence the relative ignorance of Scots of their own Celtic droving traditions and much else besides. British televi-sion has also shied away from such controversial themes in Scottish history and our school system has been slow to take full advantage of the burgeoning output of Scottish historical studies from our universities.

John Keay further suggested that from a metropolitan point-of-view,

> both the Highlands and the Wild West were frontier regions, zones of instability, anachronisms, which had not only to be settled in accordance with the norms of civilised life – the rule of law, for instance and the laws of supply and demand – but also rendered emotionally acceptable packages.

Scots like most Europeans, have lapped up the celluloid Western on offer by Hollywood as escapism, sometimes as a release from the often painful memories of their own country's past. Other Western films explored racist and class issues in the cattle ranges. *Shane* (1953) focused on the battle between small settlers and cattlemen blocking their legitimate homestead claims on public land, borrowing from the story of the Johnson County War of 1892. Even more explicitly, Michael Cimino's flawed blockbuster *Heaven's Gate* (1980) pursued the same theme, portraying the raw clash of big ranchers and the homesteaders around Buffalo, Wyoming. While Averill, Cattle Kate and Nate Champion are cast in a tragic love triangle, it catches the flow of poor immigrants from Central Europe clashing with the haughty cattle barons. Certain key characters who led the 'Invaders' are accurately portrayed and John Clay's writings are mentioned in the credits. Hollywood has explored timeless truths about Western experience, but its urban view of the conquest of the frontier has too often sought to romanticise what was ugly and unsustainable.

On both sides of the Atlantic, life was a far-from-equal struggle. Like poor American settlers, the ordinary Highland crofters and cottars were set against powerful landholding interests. Previously, Highland crofters had been compared with

American Indians. Patrick Sellar argued that Highlanders had placed themselves in the same relationship to European civilisation as the 'Aborigines of North America were to the colonists'. The sheep farmer dismissed them as anachronisms, living in turf cabins with their animals. He stated they were 'singular for patience, courage, cunning and address. Both are most virtuous where least in contact with men in a civilised state'.

The 1886 Crofting Act, an enduring monument to the Highland Land League, was the first democratic brake on untrammelled Scottish landlord power. The 1892 stand-off in Johnson County did little to postpone the victory of the powerful over the weak in the Western Civil War of Incorporation. Where hired guns failed, barbed wire, smart lawyers and political cabals succeeded. At the same time in the Wild West, Federal us laws did protect public lands and dwindling forests, promoted homesteading, restricted foreign owners and set up the world's first national parks.

Parallels between the American and Scottish experience are easy to make. The messages of Dee Brown's *Bury my Heart at Wounded Knee* (1971) and James Hunter's *Making of the Crofting Community* (1976) and his subsequent books are gradually opening a whole new debate amongst our indigenous peoples. In the Highlands ideas about increasing cattle and reducing sheep and deer on hill ground has being mooted by naturalist, John Lister-Kaye[9] and others. In the Prairie and Rocky Mountain States the idea of excluding both cattle and people and reintroducing buffalo on the open range has been put into practice by large private landholders such as media mogul, Ted Turner. It is my belief that many more people today have a readiness to reassess the episodes in our joint history. We live in a world where critics of unilateral globalisation have thrown down the gauntlet to domination by hugely powerful multi-national companies and great estates. The heirs and successors of the 1880s cattle empires are now opposed by emerging nations, voices for ecological responsibility and for strong local economies.

Short-term profiteering by flock masters effectively stole the Highlands from its indigenous cattle-rearing population and destroyed the Celtic cattle culture. Huge profits were made from mutton and wool sold to feed and clothe the urban masses before overseas supplies undercut home produce. Then sport overtook the short dominance of sheep and residual cattle production of the Highlands. Demand from the hungry industrial states of the USA and the supply of cheap beef for Europe brought the western US cattle trade to its zenith in the 1880s. In the process this destroyed a major species, the bison, and supplanted the Indians, a resource-based tribal society. Ultimately a sensible balance has to be struck on behalf of sustainable local control of resources. Drover and cowboy histories contain key lessons for those struggling to meet community needs in diverse eco-systems across the globe.

The Highland drover may have been no more wholesome than the real Rob Roy or the real Nate Champion, but the reality is far more interesting and complex than the myth. This history has brought into the foreground the drovers' part in Scotland's story and the major influences the Scottish droving tradition had on the development of huge livestock businesses across the oceans. Hopefully, they will both be better understood as a result. Droving on both sides of the Atlantic has left us a musical legacy as singers, instrumentalists and composers tap into this shared theme.

Robert Bontine Cunninghame Graham wrote in *The Horses*

of the Pampas of the music he heard in gaucho society. At wakes, 'to the light of tallow dips and the music of a cracked guitar, through the long summer nights they danced round the body of some child to celebrate his entry into Paradise.' At the crossroad stores and saloons on the plains of the young Argentine Republic, he described how the gauchos indulged in song jousting:

> ... the races at the Pulperia, the fights with the long-bladed knives for honour and a quart of wine and the long-drawn melancholy songs of the payadores, ending in a prolonged Ay.[10]

Murdo MacKenzie played his fiddle for family dances after a hard day's work in the North American cattle business. He would probably know some tunes of Niel and Nathaniel Gow, from the collection of Captain Simon Fraser of Stratherrick, of William Marshall and of his contemporary James Scott Skinner, the 'Strathspey King', as well as Anglo-American parlour music.

In saloons and bunkhouses or on the trail, migrant Scots cowboys sang ballads about being far from homes in Coigach, Tarwathie or the mountains of Kintail. While bedding down the livestock they sang about being 'all alone on the lonesome prairie'.[11] And what of John Clay? He was seen in the heyday of the Cheyenne Club beating time on the grand piano to the strains of *John Peel*!

It's hard to resist being drawn into this grand drama played out by our forebears. In our mind's eye we catch sight of a string of cattle winding through a Highland glen. They are herded by barefoot drovers, dressed in the Highland plaid, hazel stick in hand, dog at heel. The cattle, crossing the dusty Texas plains, are driven by cowboys on wiry cow-ponies, clad in Stetson, bandana and chaps with spurs a-jingling. Drover or cowboy –

in each case, they were part of a fascinating sub-culture, bit-players in a rugged physical and economic landscape.

References

1. William Forbes Skene, Celtic scholar and famine relief official in a letter to Sir Charles Trevelyan, quoted in TM Devine, *The Great Highland Famine* p 128.

2. June Skinner Sawyers, *The Complete Guide to Celtic Music* (London, Aurum Press, 2000), pp 162-91, chapter on Country Hearts, Celtic Ways.

3. Calum Iain MacLean, *The Highlands* (London, Batsford, 1959). See also Hamish Henderson, *Alias MacAlias* (Edinburgh, Polygon, 1992).

4. See sleeve notes of *Dannsa' air an drochaid* – 'Stepping on the Bridge' (CDTRAX 073 Greentrax Recordings 1994) for music by piper Hamish Moore who explores the Cape Breton legacy of the shared Celtic traditional dance culture which bridges the Atlantic.

5. David Stewart of Garth, *Sketches of the Character, Manners and Present State of the Highlanders of Scotland, with details of the Military Service of the Highland regiments* (Edinburgh 1822).

6. John Keay, *Highland Drove* (London, John Murray, 1984) p. 29.

7. Quoted by Richard White, *It's Your Misfortune and None of My Own – A New History of the American West* (Norman, University of Oklahoma University, 1991) p 621. The chapter examines ideas of the imagined West.

8. Alan le May, *The Searchers* (London & Glasgow, Fontana Books, 1956).

9. John Lister-Kaye, *Ill Fares the Land – A Sustainable Land Ethic for the Sporting Estates of the Highlands and Islands of Scotland* (Skye, Barail, 1990). Lister-Kaye's family were industrialists from Yorkshire who themselves invested in ranching on the Canadian Prairies in the cattle boom years.

10. RB Cunninghame Graham, *The Horses of the Pampas* (London,

Adam and Charles Black, 1896). Short story contained in an anthology *Father Archangel of Scotland and Other Essays* co-authored with his wife, Gabriela. Also see Grove's *Dictionary of Music and Musicians*, for explanation of South American musical styles. p.363.

11. Lines from a song *A Dream of Kintail* collected by Kenny Ross of Dingwall. The Mod Gold Medallist collected it from Cailleach NicUisdean from the Heights of Strathpeffer. It is recorded by Ceilidh Ménage on the CD *Plaids and Bandanas* BLBA 201, 1999.

Places of Interest

Scotland

The National Museum of Scotland, Edinburgh, displays the history of Scotland in chronological order from basement upwards. Cattle culture can be set in contemporary contexts. Chambers Street, Edinburgh. For details call 0131 225 7534.

The Drumlanrig's Tower Visitor Centre, Hawick, explains the history of cross-border warfare from the sixteenth century. The same building also contains the TIC. Drumlanrig's Tower, 1 Tower Knowe, High Street, Hawick TD9 9EN. For details call 01450 372547.

The Highland Folk Museum has two complementary venues. Am Fasgach, Duke Street, Kingussie, founded 1935 on a six acre site, has a museum depicting Highland life from crofter to clan chief over the past three centuries. 4 km south on the A86, the award-winning Turus Tim, Newtonmore, opened in 1998 on an eighty-acre site is an open air museum demonstrating farming methods from 1700 onwards, through practical reconstructions that capture the feel of rural life. Open May to October. For details call 01540 661307.

The Museum of Scottish Country Life, Kittockside, off Stewartfield Way, East Kilbride, Tel: 01355 224 181, a newly opened site in 2001, under the umbrella of the National Museums of Scotland; historic working farm, exhibition building, café and shop.

United States

The C M Russell Museum, Great Falls specialises in the paintings, sculptures and letters of Charlie Russell the doyen of artists who interpreted the Old West. His house and studio are incorporated on the site. 400 13th Street North, Great Falls, Montana 59401. For details call 406 727 8787.

The Jim Gatchell Memorial Museum is Buffalo's local museum that boasts 15,000 items on display. Dioramas, photographs and artefacts chronicle the history of Indian Wars, the Johnson County Invasion and much else. It comes highly recommended by the Moon Travel Handbook for Wyoming. The museum is on the corner of Main and Fort Streets, Buffalo, Wyoming. For details call 307 684 9331.

The Little Bighorn National Monument is conserved by the National Park Service, US Department of the Interior. Interpretation and tours on the extensive site of the key clash between Custer's 7th Cavalry and Crazy Horse's Indian troops in 1876. PO Box 39, Crow Agency, Montana 59022. For details call 406 638 2621.

The Buffalo Bill Historical Centre includes the Buffalo Bill Museum, Plains Indian Museum, Cody Firearms Museum, Whitney Gallery of Western Art and the McCracken Research Library and has a superb collection of Western memorabilia, images and documents. Year-round opening. 720 Sheridan Avenue, Cody, Wyoming 82414. For details call 307 587 4771.

The Autry Museum of Western Heritage holds a superb series of galleries to tell the story of the real and mythical West. It is the legacy of singing cowboy Gene Autry. Open year-round. 4700 Western Heritage Way, in Griffiths Park, Los Angeles, California 90027 USA. For details call 323 667 2000.

Canada

The Western Heritage Centre, Cochrane, Alberta, is Canada's only interactive cowboy, ranch and rodeo interpretative centre. Year-round opening, only fifteen minutes west of Calgary. An important depiction of Alberta's ranch culture. For details call 403 932 3514.

Further Reading

Magnus Magnusson and Hermann Palsson (translators), *The Vinland Sagas, The Norse Discovery of America* (London, Penguin, 1965).

Hank Wangford, *Lost Cowboys, From Patagonia to the Alamo* (London, Indigo, 1996).

Mari Sandoz, *The Cattlemen, From the Rio Grande Across the Far Marias* (Lincoln and London, University of Nebraska Press, 1958).

IF Grant, *Highland Folk Ways* (London, Routledge and Kegan Paul, 1961).

S Evans, Sarah Carter & Bill Yeo [editors], *Cowboys, Ranchers, and the Cattle Business – Cross-Border Perspectives on Ranching History* (University of Calgary Press, Alberta, 2000).

Ralph Storer, *Exploring Scottish Hill Tracks* (London, Warner Books, 1993).

Edward Buscombe, *The Searchers* (London, BFI Publishing, 2000).

Jeremy Rifkin, Beyond Beef – *The Rise and Fall of the Cattle Culture* (London, Thorsons, 1992).

ARB Haldane, *The Drove Roads of Scotland* (Edinburgh, Birlinn, 1997).

WH Murray, *Rob Roy MacGregor – His Life and Times* (Edinburgh, Canongate, 1993).

June Skinner Sawyers, *The Complete Guide to Celtic Music* (London, Aurum Press, 2000).

WM Pearce, *The Matador Land and Cattle Company* (Norman, University of Oklahoma Press, 1964).

W Turrentine Jackson, *The Enterprising Scot – Investors in the American West after 1873* (Edinburgh, Edinburgh University Press, 1968).

Tom F Cunningham, *The Diamond's Ace – Scotland and the Native Americans* (Edinburgh, Mainstream, 2001).

Richard White, *It's Your Misfortune and None of My Own – A New History of the American West* (Norman, University of Oklahoma Press, 1991).

Wayne Gard, *The Chisholm Trail* (Norman, University of Oklahoma Press, 1954).

David A Dary, *The Buffalo Book – The Full Saga of the American Animal* (Ohio, Swallow Press, 1989).

Fay E Ward, *The Cowboy at Work – All About His Job and How He Does It* (Norman, University of Oklahoma Press, 1958).

James Hunter, *Glencoe and The Indians – A Real-life Family Saga Which Spans Two Continents, Several Centuries and More Than Thirty Generations to Link Scotland's Clans With the Native Peoples of the American* West (Edinburgh, Mainstream, 1996).

Tom Smallman and Graeme Cornwallis, *Scotland – From*

Cockburnspath to the Butt of Lewis (Hawthorn, Victoria, Lonely Planet, 1999).

Don Pitcher, *Wyoming Handbook – Including Yellowstone and Grand Teton National Parks* (Chico, California, Moon Travel Handbooks, 1997).

WC McRae and Judy Jewell, *Montana Handbook – Including Glacier National Park* (Chico, California, Moon Travel Handbooks, 1999).

Andrew Hempstead, *Alberta and the Northwest Territories – Including Banff, Jasper, and the Canadian Rockies* (Chico, California, Moon Travel Handbooks, 1999).

Discography

Ceilidh Ménage, *Plaids & Bandanas, song links from Scots drovers to Wild West cowboys* (Blue Banana Music BLBA 201, 1999).

Michael Cimino's Heaven's Gate, MGM soundtrack of a United Artists Film, music to the film (Deluxe Edition, RCD 10749, 1997).

David Wilkie, *Cowboy Celtic, featuring Cowboy Celtic orchestra* (Centerfire Music, CFA006, 1996).

David Wilkie, *Cowboy Ceilidh* (Centerfire Music, CFA007, 1997).

David Wilkie, *Cowboy Celtic Collection* (Centerfire Music, licensed to Passion Music, PSA 301, 1999).

David Wilkie & Cowboy Celtic, *The Drover Road* (Centerfire Music, CFA008, 2001)

Hamish Moore, *Dannsa' Air An Drochaid (Stepping on the Bridge)* (Greentrax, CDTRAX 073, 1994).

John Watt, *Heroes* (The Living Tradition, LTCD3001, 2000). Contains two songs about Buffalo Bill visiting Dunfermline.

Woody Guthrie, *Buffalo Skinners* (The Asch Recordings Vol.4 (Smithsonian Folkways, LC 9628, 1999).

Wylie & the Wild West, *Ridin' the Hi-Line* (Rounder Records, LC 3719, 2000).

Glossary of Terms

Anglo – describes white Americans especially in the Wild West

Baile (Gaelic) – a township

Bannock (Scots) – flat, baked cake of oats, wheat, pease meal etc

Bard – a poet in Gaelic society

Chaparral (Spanish) – thick, thorny bush

Chaparejos/Chapareras (Spanish) – leather or sheepskin leg protection (diminutive pronounced 'chaps')

Coirechoille (Gaelic) – wooded corrie or hollow, placename in Lochaber probably derived from *Coir' a Choinglidh* – hollow of the defile or pass that lies south of the present day collection of buildings. (Thanks to Kate Lockhart for local knowledge).

Cinch (US) – derived from Spanish *cincha*, a girth

Creach (Gaelic) – ritual livestock raid

Dodded (Scots) – horness (cattle)

Dogone (Scots) – contemptuous term for a man

Doggone (US slang) – mild expletive

Factor (Scots) – legal manager of a landed estate on behalf of the proprietor

Gaucho (Spanish) – mestizo cowboy in Argentina

Greaser – term of abuse given by Anglo-Americans to Hispanic people

Hispanic – people of Latin American origin

Improver (Scots) – tenant or land owner who applied modern techniques on an extensive basis

Laird (Scots) – landlord

Lariat (US) – derived from Spanish *la reata* – a rope

Lazo (Spanish) – a lasso in American English, rope made of rawhide or hemp, used to capture horses and cattle.

Mart (Scots) – common abbreviation for livestock market

Mestizo (Spanish) – Indian and Spanish mixture of Latin American people

Polled (Scots) – hornless (cattle)

Quirt – derived from Spanish *quarta*, a whip

Spreidh (Gaelic) – freelance livestock raid

Tacksman (Scots) – major tenant of land on an estate who sub-let smaller tacks to clansmen and/or relations

Vaquero (Spanish) – mestizo cowboy

Index

Hansford, 108
Harrison, (US President), 116
Hatchment, A, 68
Hays, 105
Heaven's Gate, 166, 178
Hereford, 41, 53, 72, 111, 122
Herefordshire, 72, 75
Highland armies, 64
Highland cattle, 23, 37, 38, 40, 42, 43, 59, 60, 76, 163
Highland crofters, 166
Highland disorder, 32
Highland Drove, 71, 165
Highland drover, 60, 62, 65, 68, 130, 168, 170
Highland Folk Museum, 92, 172
Highland garron, 64
Highland Land League, 142, 147
Highland Man, 32
Highland Railway, 69
Highlander, The 50
Highlands and Islands, 147, 155, 162, 170
Hispanic, 130, 132, 135-137, 159-160, 179-180
Hollinshead, 34
Hollywood, 162, 164, 166
Home Rule, 77, 138, 140, 155
House of Commons, 130
House of Lords, 144
Hudson Bay Company, 84
improvement, 39-40, 43, 50, 57
Indian Territory, 87, 96
Indian War, 84, 173
Indians, 52, 79, 82, 84-86, 89, 96, 100-101, 106, 124, 130, 132-134, 137, 146, 150, 161, 163, 165, 167-168, 173, 176
Inverness-shire, 60, 141
Ireland, 23-25, 27, 32, 34, 36-38, 41, 75-78, 129, 140, 156-157
Irish cattle, 38, 59, 75-76
Irish Folklore Commission, 158
Irvine, 84, 115

Islands, 23, 28, 33, 47-48, 55, 58, 64, 71, 84, 147, 155, 162, 170
Islay, 40, 48, 55
Isle of Skye, 45
Jacobite, 32, 47, 50, 54, 72, 74-75, 89, 165
Jackson, J Turrentine, 78
James VI, 30, 53, 89
James VII, 74
John Peel, 169
Johnson County, 112, 114-115, 117, 119, 125, 167
Jura, 40, 48, 55
Kansas, 44, 62, 68, 81, 85, 96, 105, 107, 122, 124, 146, 160
Kansas Pacific, 82
Keay, John 163, 166, 170
Keir Hardie, 136
Kennedy, Lord 153, 155
Kerry, 37
King Ranch, 136
Kingussie, 172
Knockbuy, 39, 43, 48
Kyle of Lochalsh, 153
Kyle Rhea, 55
Lakota, 84-84, 150
Land League, 143, 165, 167
Leaving Coigach, 103
Lenman, Bruce 50-51
Lewis, 55, 84, 87, 153, 177
Lifting the Cattle, 29
Linton, 32, 55
Little Big Horn, 84, 150, 173
Little Bighorn National Monument, 173
Lochaber, 31, 48, 53, 59
Lochbroom, 155
Longhorn, 23, 81-2, 84, 86, 105-7
Lord Advocate, 56-7
Macdonald, Angus, 30, 84
MacDonald, Colin, 69-71
MacDonald, Sir John A, 150
MacGregor, 28, 47, 51, 53, 130, 176
MacIntyre, Duncan Ban, 162

Some other books published by **LUATH** PRESS

THE QUEST FOR

The Quest for the Celtic Key
Karen Ralls-MacLeod and
Ian Robertson
ISBN 0 946487 73 1 HB £18.99

The Quest for Arthur
Stuart McHardy
ISBN 1 842820 12 5 HB £16.99

POLITICS & CURRENT ISSUES

Scotlands of the Mind
Angus Calder
ISBN 1 84282 008 7 PB £9.99

Trident on Trial: the case for people's disarmament
Angie Zelter
ISBN 1 84282 004 4 PB £9.99

Uncomfortably Numb: A Prison Requiem
Maureen Maguire
ISBN 1 84282 001 X PB £8.99

Scotland: Land & Power – Agenda for Land Reform
Andy Wightman
ISBN 0 946487 70 7 PB £5.00

Old Scotland New Scotland
Jeff Fallow
ISBN 0 946487 40 5 PB £6.99

Some Assembly Required: Scottish Parliament
David Shepherd
ISBN 0 946487 84 7 PB £7.99

Notes from the North
Emma Wood
ISBN 0 946487 46 4 PB £8.99

NATURAL WORLD

The Hydro Boys: pioneers of renewable energy
Emma Wood
ISBN 1 84282 016 8 HB £16.99

Wild Scotland
James McCarthy
ISBN 0 946487 37 5 PB £7.50

Wild Lives: Otters – On the Swirl of the Tide
Bridget MacCaskill
ISBN 0 946487 67 7 PB £9.99

Wild Lives: Foxes – The Blood is Wild
Bridget MacCaskill
ISBN 0 946487 71 5 PB £9.99

Scotland – Land & People: An Inhabited Solitude
James McCarthy
ISBN 0 946487 57 X PB £7.99

The Highland Geology Trail
John L Roberts
ISBN 0 946487 36 7 PB £4.99

'Nothing but Heather!'
Gerry Cambridge
ISBN 0 946487 49 9 PB £15.00

Red Sky at Night
John Barrington
ISBN 0 946487 60 X PB £8.99

Listen to the Trees
Don MacCaskill
ISBN 0 946487 65 0 PB £9.99

ISLANDS

The Islands that Roofed the World: Easdale, Belnahua, Luing & Seil:
Mary Withall
ISBN 0 946487 76 6 PB £4.99

Rum: Nature's Island
Magnus Magnusson
ISBN 0 946487 32 4 PB £7.95

LUATH GUIDES TO SCOTLAND

The North West Highlands: Roads to the Isles
Tom Atkinson
ISBN 0 946487 54 5 PB £4.95

Mull and Iona: Highways and Byways
Peter Macnab
ISBN 0 946487 58 8 PB £4.95

The Northern Highlands: The Empty Lands
Tom Atkinson
ISBN 0 946487 55 3   PB £4.95

The West Highlands: The Lonely Lands
Tom Atkinson
ISBN 0 946487 56 1 PB £4.95

South West Scotland
Tom Atkinson
ISBN 0 946487 04 9 PB £4.95

TRAVEL & LEISURE

Die Kleine Schottlandfibel [Scotland Guide in German]
Hans-Walter Arends
ISBN 0 946487 89 8 PB £8.99

Let's Explore Edinburgh Old Town
Anne Bruce English
ISBN 0 946487 98 7 PB £4.99

Edinburgh's Historic Mile
Duncan Priddle
ISBN 0 946487 97 9 PB £2.99

Pilgrims in the Rough: St Andrews beyond the 19th hole
Michael Tobert
ISBN 0 946487 74 X PB £7.99

FOOD & DRINK

The Whisky Muse: Scotch whisky in poem & song
various, ed. Robin Laing
ISBN 0 946487 95 2 PB £12.99

First Foods Fast: good simple baby meals
Lara Boyd
ISBN 1 84282 002 8 PB £4.99

Edinburgh and Leith Pub Guide
Stuart McHardy
ISBN 0 946487 80 4 PB £4.95

WALK WITH LUATH

Skye 360: walking the coastline of Skye
Andrew Dempster
ISBN 0 946487 85 5 PB £8.99

Walks in the Cairngorms
Ernest Cross
ISBN 0 946487 09 X PB £4.95

Short Walks in the Cairngorms
Ernest Cross
ISBN 0 946487 23 5 PB £4.95

The Joy of Hillwalking
Ralph Storer
ISBN 0 946487 28 6 PB £7.50

Scotland's Mountains before the Mountaineers
Ian R Mitchell
ISBN 0 946487 39 1 PB £9.99

Mountain Days and Bothy Nights
Dave Brown and Ian R Mitchell
ISBN 0 946487 15 4 PB £7.50

SPORT

Ski & Snowboard Scotland
Hilary Parke
ISBN 0 946487 35 9 PB £6.99

Over the Top with the Tartan Army
Andy McArthur
ISBN 0 946487 45 6 PB £7.99

BIOGRAPHY

The Last Lighthouse
Sharma Krauskopf
ISBN 0 946487 96 0 PB £7.99

Tobermory Teuchter
Peter Macnab
ISBN 0 946487 41 3 PB £7.99

Bare Feet and Tackety Boots
Archie Cameron
ISBN 0 946487 17 0 PB £7.95

Come Dungeons Dark
John Taylor Caldwell
ISBN 0 946487 19 7 PB £6.95

HISTORY

Civil Warrior
Robin Bell
ISBN 1 84282 013 3 HB £10.99

A Passion for Scotland
David R Ross
ISBN 1 84282 019 2 PB £5.99

Reportage Scotland
Louise Yeoman
ISBN 0 946487 61 8 PB £9.99

Blind Harry's Wallace
Hamilton of Gilbert-
ISBN 0 946487 33 2 PB £8.99

Blind Harry's Wallace
field [intro/ed Elspeth King]
ISBN 0 946487 43 X HB £15.00

SOCIAL HISTORY

Pumpherston: the story of a shale oil village
Sybil Cavanagh
ISBN 1 84282 011 7 HB £17.99

Pumpherston: the story of a shale oil village
Sybil Cavanagh
ISBN 1 84282 015 X PB £7.99

Shale Voices
Alistair Findlay
ISBN 0 946487 78 2 HB £17.99

Shale Voices
Alistair Findlay
ISBN 0 946487 63 4 PB £10.99

A Word for Scotland
Jack Campbell
ISBN 0 946487 48 0 PB £12.99

ON THE TRAIL OF

On the Trail of William Wallace
David R Ross
ISBN 0 946487 47 2 PB £7.99

On the Trail of Robert the Bruce
David R Ross
ISBN 0 946487 52 9 PB £7.99

On the Trail of Mary Queen of Scots
J Keith Cheetham
ISBN 0 946487 50 2 PB £7.99

On the Trail of Bonnie Prince Charlie
David R Ross
ISBN 0 946487 68 5 PB £7.99

On the Trail of Robert Burns
John Cairney
ISBN 0 946487 51 0 PB £7.99

On the Trail of John Muir
Cherry Good
ISBN 0 946487 62 6 PB £7.99

On the Trail of Queen Victoria in the Highlands
Ian R Mitchell
ISBN 0 946487 79 0 PB £7.99

On the Trail of Robert Service
G Wallace Lockhart
ISBN 0 946487 24 3 PB £7.99

On the Trail of the Pilgrim Fathers
J Keith Cheetham
ISBN 0 946487 83 9 PB £7.99

FOLKLORE

Scotland: Myth, Legend & Folklore
Stuart McHardy
ISBN 0 946487 69 3 PB £7.99

Luath Storyteller: Highland Myths & Legends
George W Macpherson
ISBN 1 84282 003 6 PB £5.00

Tales of the North Coast
Alan Temperley
ISBN 0 946487 18 9 PB £8.99

Tall Tales from an Island
Peter Macnab
ISBN 0 946487 07 3 PB £8.99

The Supernatural Highlands
Francis Thompson
ISBN 0 946487 31 6 PB £8.99

GENEALOGY

Scottish Roots: step-by-step guide for ancestor hunters
Alwyn James
ISBN 1 84282 007 9 PB £9.99

WEDDINGS, MUSIC AND DANCE

The Scottish Wedding Book
G Wallace Lockhart
ISBN 1 94282 010 9 PB £12.99

Fiddles and Folk
G Wallace Lockhart
ISBN 0 946487 38 3 PB £7.95

Highland Balls and Village Halls
G Wallace Lockhart
ISBN 0 946487 12 X PB £6.95

POETRY

Bad Ass Raindrop
Kokumo Rocks
ISBN 1 84282 018 4 PB £6.99

Caledonian Cramboclink: the Poetry of
William Neill
ISBN 0 946487 53 7 PB £8.99

Men and Beasts: wild men & tame animals
Val Gillies & Rebecca Marr
ISBN 0 946487 92 8 PB £15.00

Luath Burns Companion
John Cairney
ISBN 1 84282 000 1 PB £10.00

Scots Poems to be read aloud
intro Stuart McHardy
ISBN 0 946487 81 2 PB £5.00

Poems to be read aloud
various
ISBN 0 946487 00 6 PB £5.00

CARTOONS

Broomie Law
Cinders McLeod
ISBN 0 946487 99 5 PB £4.00

FICTION

The Road Dance
John MacKay
ISBN 1 84282 024 9 PB £9.99

Milk Treading
Nick Smith
ISBN 0 946487 75 8 PB £9.99

The Strange Case of RL Stevenson
Richard Woodhead
ISBN 0 946487 86 3 HB £16.99

But n Ben A-Go-Go
Matthew Fitt
ISBN 1 84282 014 1 PB £6.99

But n Ben A-Go-Go
Matthew Fitt
ISBN 0 946487 82 0 HB £10.99

Grave Robbers
Robin Mitchell
ISBN 0 946487 72 3 PB £7.99

The Bannockburn Years
William Scott
ISBN 0 946487 34 0 PB £7.95

The Great Melnikov
Hugh MacLachlan
ISBN 0 946487 42 1 PB £7.95

LANGUAGE

Luath Scots Language Learner [Book]
L Colin Wilson
ISBN 0 946487 91 X PB £9.99

Luath Scots Language Learner [Double Audio CD Set]
L Colin Wilson
ISBN 1 84282 026 5 CD £16.99

Luath Press Limited
committed to publishing well written books worth reading

LUATH PRESS takes its name from Robert Burns, whose little collie
Luath (*Gael.,* swift or nimble) tripped up Jean Armour at a wedding and gave
him the chance to speak to the woman who was to be his wife and
the abiding love of his life. Burns called one of *The Twa
Dogs* Luath after Cuchullin's hunting dog in *Ossian's
Fingal.* Luath Press grew up in the heart of Burns
country, and now resides a few steps up the road
from Burns' first lodgings in Edinburgh's Royal
Mile.
Luath offers you distinctive writing with a hint
of unexpected pleasures.

Most UK bookshops either carry our books in
stock or can order them for you. To order direct
from us, please send a £sterling cheque, postal order,
international money order or your credit card details
(number, address of cardholder and expiry date) to us at the
address below. Please add post and packing as follows: UK
– £1.00 per delivery address; overseas surface mail – £2.50
per delivery address; overseas airmail – £3.50 for the first book to each delivery address, plus £1.00 for each additional book by airmail to the same
address. If your order is a gift, we will happily enclose your card or message
at no extra charge.

Luath Press Limited
543/2 Castlehill
The Royal Mile
Edinburgh EH1 2ND
Scotland
Telephone: 0131 225 4326 (24 hours)
Fax: 0131 225 4324
email: gavin.macdougall@luath.co.uk
Website: www.luath.co.uk